THE OFFICIAL
STRANGER THINGS COOKBOOK

JOSHUA DAVID STEIN

WITH RECIPES BY SUSAN VU

RANDOM HOUSE
WORLDS

NEW YORK

Random House Worlds
An imprint of Random House
A division of Penguin Random House LLC
1745 Broadway, New York, NY 10019
randomhousebooks.com
penguinrandomhouse.com

Hardcover ISBN 978-1-9848-6162-7
Ebook ISBN 978-1-9848-6163-4

Printed in Canada

2 4 6 8 9 7 5 3 1

First Edition

Editor: Sarah Malarkey
Production editor: Abby Duval
Managing editor: Susan Seeman
Designer: Laura Palese
Creative director: Jenny Davis
Art director: Ian Dingman
Production manager: Mark Maguire
Prepress color manager: Richard Booth
Food photographer: Kristin Teig
Food stylist: Monica Pierini | Food stylist assistant: Alyssa Kondracki
Prop stylist: Martha Bernabe | Prop stylist assistants: Laila Ibrahim, Crystal Simon
Photo retoucher: Ché Graham
Recipe developer: Susan Vu
Copy editor: Leda Scheintaub | Proofreaders: Pat Dailey, Zora O'Neill,
Darcie Robertson, Tess Rossi, Caryl Weintraub
Indexer: Gina Guilinger

Waffle illustration on cover and page 1: Butcher Billy
Stock images: lined spiralbound paper—ninjaMonkeyStudio/Getty;
sky with birds and rainbows—fumiko Inoue/Getty; ripped newspaper—scol22/Getty;
restaurant guest check—THEPALMER/Getty; weathered paper—paladin13/Getty; vintage
stickers—Kwangmoozaa/Getty; creased paper—asimetric/Getty;
crinkled binder paper—smartstock/Getty; graph paper—belterz/Getty;
checkered racing background—sldesign78/Getty; old blank postcard—kyoshino/Getty;
blue notebook paper—hudiemm/Getty; blank vintage postcard—darkbird77/Getty;
beige vintage paper—tomograf/Getty; black grit background—kosmofish/Shutterstock;
green dot matrix paper—hudiemm/Getty

The authorized representative in the EU for product safety and compliance is
Penguin Random House Ireland, Morrison Chambers, 32 Nassau Street,
Dublin D02 YH68, Ireland. https://eu-contact.penguin.ie

HOW TO USE THIS BOOK

There's no wrong way to use the recipes from this book. They are organized chronologically, from the years 1983 to 1987, to best create the world of Hawkins (and beyond) as we see it during the five seasons of the show. Within that, we've loosely followed the chronology of events. (For instance, Murray's Risotto comes *before* Yuri's Peanut Butter Blossom cookies in chapter four, 1986.) Typically, each chapter starts with breakfast and moves through to lunch, dinner, and dessert.

What if you're hungry for breakfast (or lunch or dinner)? Well, here are all the recipes categorized by how they fall in the day.

DESSERTS

DRINKS

APPOINTMENT COOKING
(like appointment viewing but with food)

Say you want to throw a *Stranger Things* party. Great! Invite your friends over for some . . .

Cuddle up for a family movie night with . . .

Relive the glory of the mall food court with an homage to Starcourt . . .

CHAPTER ONE

LIKE MANY SMALL TOWNS across America, Hawkins, Indiana, is full of families around their dinner tables, dens with the television on, and well-used home kitchens. Sure, there's a secret government laboratory, staffed by nefarious scientists hell-bent on opening a portal into the demonic realm called the Upside Down, but the families gathered in their living rooms don't know about that. (Well, at least most of them don't. At least for now.)

What the families of Hawkins know are the smells of home cooking. As the setting sun streams through the forest near Mirkwood, the scents of dinner waft from nearby homes, forming a cloud of comfort that, more than a dinner bell or a shout, lure Hawkins' children back home to the glow of the dining room. For Nancy, Mike, and baby Holly, these comforts are Karen Wheeler's delicious dinners, casseroles of great achievement, and salads of sophistication. For Will, it's the quick weekday suppers his mother, Joyce, makes after she returns from her shift at Melvald's, and sometimes the breakfasts his older brother, Jonathan, prepares. For Dustin, it's Claudia Henderson's comfort food. The food isn't always fancy, but it is delicious and it's made with love.

There are of course restaurants: old standbys like Benny's Burgers, serving Hawkins since 1956 from its humble location on Randolph Lane, and the red-sauce joint Enzo's, one of the town's nicest restaurants. (Main Street is happily free from fast food chains.) And as Mike, Lucas, Dustin, Will, and the rest of Hawkins Middle School students will tell you, there's a school cafeteria too. The less said about it the better, except for its truly exceptional chocolate pudding.

As 1983 opens, Hawkins is a town full of happy home cooks, where dinners are a chance to come together as a family, where recipes are traded, and where no one could ever suspect the life-or-death drama that awaits.

RECIPES

Jonathan's Scrambled Eggs

SERVES 4

These simple but delicious scrambled eggs have been a Byers family favorite ever since Will could remember. Especially now that both boys are in school and Joyce is often at work, they're a life- and time-saving breakfast.

8 eggs
¼ cup / 60ml milk
Kosher salt and freshly ground black pepper
3 tablespoons unsalted butter
Toasted bread, for serving

Optional add-ins

1 tablespoon chopped fresh soft herbs, such as flat-leaf parsley or basil

1 tablespoon chopped scallions

2 tablespoons chopped crispy bacon

¼ cup / 25g your favorite shredded cheese, such as sharp cheddar or mozzarella

½ cup sauteed sliced mushrooms (30g), diced bell pepper (75g), or baby spinach (10g)

1. In a large bowl, combine the eggs and milk, season with salt and pepper, and whisk vigorously until pale yellow in color and almost foamy. Set aside.

2. In a large nonstick skillet over medium heat, melt the butter until it starts to lightly bubble and become foamy. Add the eggs and cook, using a heat-resistant rubber spatula to gently stir and scrape as needed, until large, fluffy curds form, 4 to 7 minutes. If using any optional add-ins, pull the eggs off the heat a minute before they have finished cooking and fold the add-in(s) into the soft eggs and cook in the residual heat until warmed through (or, in the case of the cheese, melted).

3. Divide the scrambled eggs among four serving plates and serve immediately with toasted bread.

Hawkins PD Glazed Donuts

MAKES 13 DONUTS (A BAKER'S DOZEN)

Much to Florence's displeasure, the Hawkins Police Department runs on donuts. She knows that when Hop is in a bad mood—which he frequently is—the only thing to soothe him is a cup of bitter burning brew and a glazed donut, preferably still warm. He and the rest of the station go through a dozen a day, easy. But, like the caring secretary she is, Flo occasionally sneaks in a healthier vegan alternative, especially in the fall, using local pumpkins from the McCorkle Farm. She hasn't heard any complaints yet.

Donuts

¼ cup / 60ml warm water (110°F to 115°F / 43°C to 46°C)

¾ teaspoon granulated sugar, plus ⅓ cup / 65g, divided

1 (¼-ounce / 7g) packet active dry yeast

½ cup / 120ml half-and-half or whole milk, at room temperature

2 double shots of good espresso (about ½ cup / 4 ounces), at room temperature

2 large eggs, at room temperature

1 large egg yolk, at room temperature

1¼ teaspoons kosher salt

4½ cups / 630g all-purpose flour, divided, plus more for dusting

¼ cup / 55g unsalted butter, cut into ½-inch / 1.3cm cubes and softened

Vegetable oil, for coating bowl and frying

Cooking spray

Glaze

⅓ cup / 80ml half-and-half

⅓ cup / 80ml water, plus more if needed

½ teaspoon vanilla extract

¼ teaspoon kosher salt

3½ cups / 420g confectioners' sugar

Special Equipment

One 3-inch / 7.5cm donut cutter or one 3-inch / 7.5cm round cutter and one 1-inch / 2.5cm round cutter

1. Make the donuts: Put the warm water in a stand mixer bowl fitted with the whisk attachment. Stir in ¾ teaspoon of the granulated sugar and the active dry yeast and let sit until foamy, about 5 minutes.

2. To the bloomed yeast mixture, add the remaining ⅓ cup / 65g granulated sugar, the half-and-half, espresso, eggs, egg yolk, and salt. On low speed, mix until smooth and well combined (alternatively, you can just whisk the wet ingredients by hand). Switch over to the dough hook and turn the speed to medium. Gradually add 4¼ cups / 595g of the flour, ¼ cup / 35g at a time, and continue mixing until the mixture comes together to form a shaggy dough, about 2 minutes, scraping down the sides of the bowl as needed. With the mixer running, gradually add the butter, 2 to 3 cubes at a time, until blended into the dough, about 3 minutes.

3. Once all of the butter has been added, increase the speed to medium-high and continue mixing until the dough is only slightly tacky to the touch (it should not feel super sticky or greasy) and mostly gathers around the hook (depending on how deep your mixer bowl is, a little bit of tacky dough on the bottom is okay), 5 to 8 additional minutes, scraping down the sides of the bowl as needed. If after 5 minutes the dough is still very sticky and not wrapping around the hook, start adding in the remaining flour, a tablespoon at a time, to help move it along. Remove the bowl and dough hook from the stand mixer (leaving the dough on the hook).

RECIPE CONTINUES >>>

"MORNINGS ARE FOR COFFEE AND CONTEMPLATION."

HOPPER

4. Pour a small splash of vegetable oil into a large bowl, then use your hands to rub it evenly inside the bowl. With your greased hands, remove the dough from the hook and the stand mixer bowl, form it into a rough ball, and transfer the dough into the greased bowl. Turn the dough to coat it in the oil, cover the bowl with plastic wrap, and let rise in a warm place until doubled in size, 1 to 1½ hours.

5. Line a baking sheet with parchment paper and lightly coat with cooking spray; set aside. Turn the dough out onto a lightly floured surface and roll out into a ½-inch / 1.3cm-thick round (about 12 inches / 30cm around). Dip a 3-inch / 7.5cm donut cutter into flour, then use it to cut out ten or eleven donuts (dipping the cutter in more flour in between each cut). Alternatively, you can cut out the donuts using a 3-inch / 7.5cm round cutter and a 1-inch / 2.5cm round cutter. Arrange the donuts and donut holes on the prepared baking sheet, leaving space between each. Re-roll the scraps (about a 7½-inch / 19cm wide round) to get two or three additional donuts and donut holes, for a total of thirteen (a baker's dozen!). Cover loosely with plastic wrap and set aside at room temperature until slightly puffed and when you press your finger lightly into the dough, it springs back slowly, 30 to 45 minutes.

6. Heat 2 inches / 5cm of vegetable oil in a large Dutch oven or heavy-bottomed pot over medium-high heat until a deep-fry thermometer registers 340°F / 171°C.

7. As the oil is heating up, line a large baking sheet with a couple layers of paper towels. Use kitchen shears to cut the parchment paper around each donut, leaving a ½-inch / 1.3cm border around the dough.

8. When the oil is at temperature, carefully invert three or four donuts into the oil and peel off the parchment with tongs. Fry until golden on the first side, about 1 minute, use a slotted spoon to flip the donuts over, and fry until golden on the second side, about 1 minute. Flip once more and cook for an additional minute, using the slotted spoon to gently push down on the donuts as they fry so that both sides get even color. Transfer to the prepared baking sheet. Bring the oil back to 340°F / 171°C and repeat with the remaining donuts. Once all of the donuts have been fried, use your hands to carefully add the donut holes to the oil and fry, stirring occasionally, until puffed and golden brown, about 2 minutes. Transfer to the baking sheet lined with paper towels. Set aside while you make the glaze.

9. Make the glaze: Set two wire racks over two rimmed baking sheets and set aside.

10. In a medium saucepan set over low heat, combine the half-and-half, water, vanilla, and salt and warm until hot and steamy, 1 to 2 minutes. Remove from the heat, add the confectioners' sugar, and whisk until melted and the mixture forms a thin glaze.

11. Add one warm donut to the warm glaze and use two wooden chopsticks or thick skewers to help you coat the donut in the glaze, turning and pushing the donut to the sides of the pan as needed. Use the chopsticks or skewers to transfer the glazed donut to the wire rack. Repeat until all of the donuts are coated in glaze. Add the donut holes to the remaining glaze in the saucepan and turn to coat completely. Pour the donut holes and glaze onto an empty part of one of the wire racks. Allow the glaze to set completely at room temperature, about 30 minutes, then serve.

Florence's Vegan Pumpkin Donuts

MAKES 12 DONUTS

Cooking spray
⅔ cup / 160ml unsweetened soy milk, plus
    2 to 6 teaspoons, divided
2 teaspoons fresh lemon juice
½ cup / 50g raw shelled black walnuts
    see Cook's Note
1¼ cups / 175g all-purpose flour
½ cup / 70g whole wheat flour
1½ teaspoons ground cinnamon
½ teaspoon ground ginger
¼ teaspoon ground allspice
¼ teaspoon freshly grated nutmeg
1 teaspoon baking powder
½ teaspoon baking soda
½ teaspoon kosher salt
1 cup / 228g homemade or store-bought
    pure pumpkin puree
¾ cup / 150g packed light brown sugar
¼ cup / 60ml extra-virgin olive oil
2 teaspoons vanilla extract
1½ cups / 180g confectioners' sugar
3 tablespoons pure maple syrup

Special Equipment
2 (6-cavity) donut baking pans

Black walnut trees can be found statewide in Indiana, and the nuts are known for their rich, bold flavor. If you can't find them, you can use English walnuts instead, which are more readily available if you live outside Indiana.

1. Preheat the oven to 375°F / 190°C. Spray 2 (6-cavity) donut baking pans with cooking spray and place a wire rack on top of a baking sheet. Set aside.

2. In a medium bowl, combine ⅔ cup / 160ml of the soy milk with the lemon juice and stir to combine. The lemon juice will cause the soy milk to curdle and make vegan "buttermilk." Set aside while you toast the walnuts.

3. Scatter the walnuts onto a small baking sheet and toast in the oven until lightly browned and fragrant, 7 to 9 minutes, stirring the nuts several times to ensure they toast evenly. Transfer the nuts to a cutting board to cool completely, then finely chop and set aside.

4. In a large bowl, whisk together the all-purpose flour, whole wheat flour, cinnamon, ground ginger, allspice, nutmeg, baking powder, baking soda, and salt. In the bowl with the vegan "buttermilk," add the pumpkin puree, brown sugar, olive oil, and vanilla. Whisk until smooth. Add to the flour mixture and whisk until mostly combined, then switch over to a rubber spatula and mix until just combined. Transfer the batter into a large resealable plastic storage bag.

5. Cut a 1-inch / 2.5cm opening in one corner of the bag and pipe the batter evenly into the prepared donut baking pans, filling each cavity about two-thirds full.

6. Bake until puffed and a toothpick inserted into a donut comes out clean, 12 to 14 minutes. Cool in the pans for 5 minutes, then carefully remove the donuts from the pans and place them smooth-side up on the wire rack to cool completely.

7. In a medium bowl, combine the confectioners' sugar, maple syrup, and 2 teaspoons of the remaining soy milk. Whisk until completely smooth. The consistency should be thick but pourable, similar to glue. Whisk in additional soy milk, ½ teaspoon at a time, until you reach that consistency.

8. Once the donuts are cooled, dip the smooth side of the donuts into the glaze and allow any excess to drip off. As you glaze the donuts, immediately sprinkle the tops with the chopped walnuts, then return the donuts to the wire rack. Allow the glaze to set at room temperature, then serve immediately.

9. The donuts are best enjoyed the same day they are baked, but you can transfer any leftover donuts to an airtight container and store at room temperature for up to 3 days. The frosting will absorb into the donuts as they sit, but they will still taste delicious.

Snacks for Castle Byers

Waging a campaign can be hard work, and the Party needs sustenance as Will, Mike, Dustin, and Lucas embark upon their quest to defeat the Demogorgon. Thankfully, Joyce provides the snacks for Castle Byers, deep in the woods—along with some rules, of course.

Castle Byers Trail Mix

MAKES ABOUT 6 CUPS / 665G

2 cups / 70g mini pretzel twists
1 cup / 140g roasted and salted almonds
1 cup / 120g roasted and salted peanuts
½ cup / 90g milk chocolate chips
½ cup / 100g candy-coated chocolate candies
½ cup / 70g raisins
½ cup / 75g roasted and salted shelled sunflower
   seeds

1. In a large bowl, combine the pretzel twists, almonds, peanuts, chocolate chips, chocolate candies, raisins, and sunflower seeds and stir to incorporate.

2. Serve immediately or transfer to an airtight container and store at room temperature for up to 1 month.

Peanut Butter Trail Mix Bars

MAKES 12 BARS

Cooking spray
½ cup / 120g smooth peanut butter
¼ cup / 50g packed dark brown sugar
¼ cup / 60ml honey
3 tablespoons unsalted butter
3 cups / 333g Castle Byers Trail Mix (preceding
   recipe)
1½ cups / 150g rolled oats, divided

1. Lightly coat a 9-inch / 23cm-square baking pan with cooking spray, then line with two overlapping pieces of parchment paper that go up the sides of the pan. Set aside.

2. In a small saucepan over medium heat, combine the peanut butter, brown sugar, honey, and butter. Cook, stirring frequently, until the mixture is smooth and starts to lightly bubble, 4 to 6 minutes. Continue to cook, stirring constantly, for 2 minutes more, then immediately transfer to a large bowl. Set aside to cool slightly.

3. Using your hands, lightly break up any pretzels in the trail mix, then add the trail mix to a food processor, along with ½ cup / 50g of the oats. Pulse until coarsely chopped (some nuts and chocolate pieces will remain whole, and that is okay). Add the remaining 1 cup / 100g oats to the peanut butter–honey mixture and stir to combine (this helps to cool down the mixture so that the chocolate doesn't melt when added). Add the chopped trail mix and stir again until well combined.

4. Scrape the mixture into the prepared baking pan and flatten using the back of a rubber spatula or measuring cup. Make sure to press down on the mixture evenly and firmly because that will make cutting the bars much easier. Refrigerate until completely chilled and set, about 2 hours. Using the parchment paper, lift the large trail mix bar from the pan and then use a serrated knife to cut into twelve individual bars.

5. Serve the bars immediately or transfer to an airtight container and store in the refrigerator for up to 2 weeks.

RECIPE CONTINUES ›››

Loaded Oatmeal Trail Mix Cookies

MAKES 15 OR 16 COOKIES

1½ cups / 150g rolled oats, divided
⅓ cup / 45g all-purpose flour
½ teaspoon baking soda
¼ teaspoon kosher salt
¾ cup / 150g packed dark brown sugar
½ cup / 110g unsalted butter, at room temperature
1 egg, at room temperature
2 teaspoons vanilla extract
1½ cups / 166g Castle Byers Trail Mix (page 25), coarsely chopped

1. In a blender, combine 1¼ cups / 125g of the oats and the flour and blend until very finely ground. Transfer to a medium bowl and add the baking soda and salt. Whisk to combine, then set aside.

2. In a large bowl, combine the brown sugar and butter. Using an electric handheld mixer on low speed, incorporate the sugar into the butter. Turn the speed to medium-high and blend until pale and fluffy, about 5 minutes, scraping down the bowl as needed. Add the egg and vanilla and mix until smooth and creamy, 30 seconds to 1 minute more. Add the oat-flour mixture and mix on low speed until just combined. Add the trail mix and remaining ¼ cup / 25g oats and stir into the dough by hand using a rubber spatula. Cover the bowl with plastic wrap and chill in the refrigerator for 1 hour.

3. Preheat the oven to 375°F / 190°C. Line two baking sheets with parchment paper.

4. Working with half of the chilled dough, scoop out a portion of about 3 tablespoons. Gently roll into a ball and place it on one of the prepared baking sheets. Continue to do this. You should have eight balls; arrange them so they are spaced evenly apart. Place the unportioned dough back in the refrigerator.

5. Bake the cookies until they are golden brown around the edges but still appear slightly underdone in the center, rotating the baking sheet 180 degrees halfway through, 10 to 12 minutes. Let cool for 5 minutes on the baking sheet, then transfer to a wire rack to cool completely. The cookies will puff in the oven but deflate slightly while cooling.

6. As the first batch of cookies is cooling, roll the remaining dough into balls and arrange on the second baking sheet. Repeat the baking and cooling process.

7. Once cooled, serve the cookies immediately or transfer to an airtight container and store at room temperature for up to 5 days.

Snacks for Castle Byers!

Eat them all or take them back home. We don't want any bears visiting.

MEMORIES

Demogorgonzola Cheese Puffs

MAKES 18 CHEESE PUFFS

Terrifying, evil, and delicious? Sure, the Demogorgon is terrorizing the inhabitants of Hawkins, snatching innocent children and spiriting them into the Upside Down. But that doesn't mean the Demogorgon can't be a muse for this decadent hors d'oeuvre. Utilizing a mixture of cheeses (cream, mozzarella, gorgonzola), these semi-gorgonzola cheese puffs are as addictive as the Demogorgon is scary. As the pastry shells open, they mimic the terrifying flower-face of the creature, while the pomegranate seeds resemble the nefarious monster's dentistry.

8 ounces / 225g cream cheese, at room temperature

¾ cup / 75g shredded whole milk, low-moisture mozzarella cheese

⅔ cup / 90g crumbled gorgonzola cheese

2 tablespoons sliced fresh chives

¼ teaspoon granulated garlic

Freshly ground black pepper

2 teaspoons unsalted butter

1 ripe Bartlett or D'Anjou pear, peeled, cored, and finely diced

Pinch of kosher salt

¼ cup / 60ml dry white wine

1½ tablespoons granulated sugar

1 cup / 100g raw walnuts

1 egg

All-purpose flour, for dusting

3 puff pastry sheets, thawed

½ cup / 80g pomegranate seeds

Special Equipment
1 (5-inch / 13cm) star cookie cutter

1. In a medium bowl, stir together the cream cheese, mozzarella, gorgonzola, chives, granulated garlic, and several grinds of black pepper. Chill the cheese mixture in the refrigerator until it becomes firm enough to roll into balls, about 30 minutes.

2. Position two racks in the upper and lower center of the oven and preheat to 375°F / 190°C.

3. In a small sauté pan, melt the butter over medium heat. Add the pear and salt and cook, stirring frequently, until crisp-tender, about 5 minutes. Add the white wine and sugar. Raise the heat slightly and bring to a strong simmer, stirring occasionally, about 2 minutes. Continue to simmer, stirring occasionally, until the pear is tender and all of the wine has evaporated, 7 to 10 minutes. Transfer to a small bowl and cool completely at room temperature.

4. Scatter the walnuts onto a small baking sheet and toast on the upper rack of the oven until lightly browned and fragrant, 7 to 9 minutes, stirring the nuts several times to ensure they toast evenly. Transfer the nuts to a cutting board to cool completely, then chop very finely. Place the chopped walnuts onto a small plate and set aside. Wipe the baking sheet clean and set aside.

5. Raise the oven temperature to 400°F / 200°C. Line two baking sheets with parchment paper.

6. Use a tablespoon to portion out and roll the cheese mixture into eighteen equal balls (1 heaping tablespoon per ball). Roll the cheese balls in the chopped walnuts until well coated, then transfer to the small baking sheet you used to toast the walnuts. Chill the cheese balls in the refrigerator while you prepare the puff pastry.

7. In a small bowl, whisk together the egg and a splash of water. Scatter a thin layer of flour onto a small plate and set aside. On a lightly floured work surface, roll out one puff pastry sheet (keep the other two puff pastry sheets in the refrigerator

RECIPE CONTINUES »»

until you're ready to roll and cut them) into an 11-inch / 28cm square. Dip a large star cookie cutter into the flour on the plate and use the cutter to cut out five stars from the puff pastry. Separate the excess pastry from the stars and press together enough of the pastry scraps (just press the dough together and do not re-roll because that will cause the pastry to become tough) so one additional star can be cut out, for a total of six stars from the first pastry sheet. Repeat the rolling and cutting with the two remaining pastry sheets, so you end up with eighteen stars. Save any excess pastry for another use if desired.

8. Place 1½ teaspoons of the cooked pear in the center of a puff pastry star and top with a cheese ball. Brush the points of the stars with some of the egg wash, then wrap each of the five points up and over the cheese ball so they just touch—but do not press the points together. Gently pick up the wrapped cheese ball, holding the bottom with one hand, and use your fingers to push in any edges at the bottom of the puff pastry to create a rounded bottom that clings to the cheese ball. Place the formed cheese ball onto one of the prepared baking sheets. Repeat to make seventeen additional puff pastry–covered cheese balls (nine per baking sheet). Once the first baking sheet is filled with nine cheese balls, chill that baking sheet in the refrigerator while you work on filling the second baking sheet.

9. Brush the outside of each puff pastry–covered cheese ball with more egg wash and bake, rotating the baking sheets top to bottom and front to back after 8 minutes, until the pastry is puffed and deeply browned in spots, 15 to 18 minutes. As the puff pastry bakes up around the cheese balls, some of the points will stay up and some will open. Remove from the oven and let cool on the baking sheets for 5 minutes. Insert pomegranate seeds into any of the cheese that peeks through the puff pastry, then transfer the cheese puffs to a large serving platter and serve immediately.

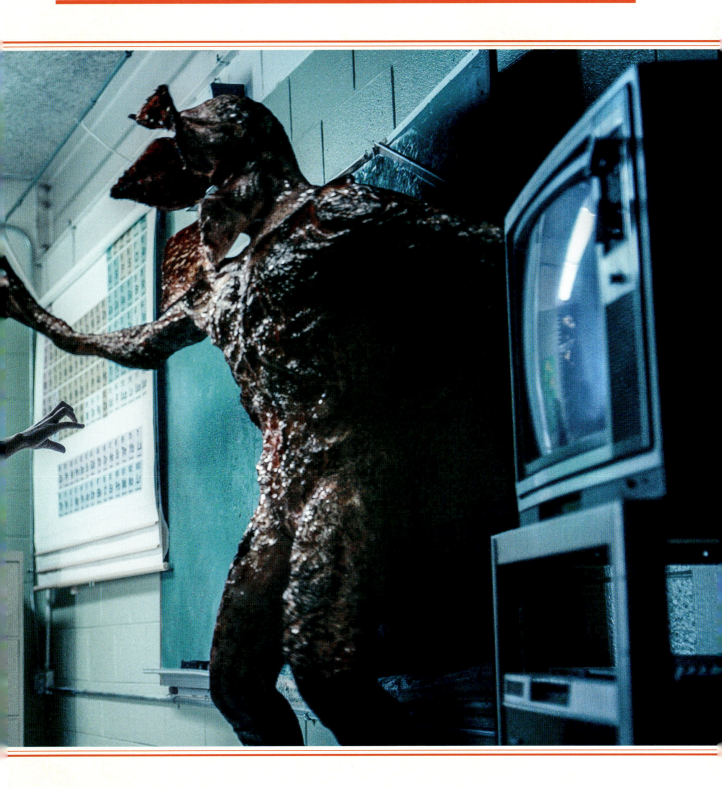

Benny's Famous Burger and French Fries

Benny's Burgers is a classic American diner, presided over by the gruff but kindhearted Benny. It's not a fancy place, but it is a good one, and it's home to Hawkins' best cheeseburger and fries. Like any great diner, the booths at Benny's hold a cross section of Hawkins: cops, hairstylists, high school kids on dates, and—for a while—a very scared little girl who escaped from the laboratory. They all love Benny, and most of all, they love his burger.

Benny's Burger

SERVES 4

Cajun Seasoning

2 teaspoons smoked paprika
1½ teaspoons granulated garlic
1 teaspoon granulated onion
1 teaspoon dried thyme
1 teaspoon dried oregano
½ teaspoon cayenne pepper
2 teaspoons kosher salt
½ teaspoon freshly ground black pepper

Rémoulade

½ teaspoon granulated garlic
½ cup / 120g mayonnaise
1 tablespoon finely chopped fresh flat-leaf parsley
1 tablespoon thinly sliced scallions (green parts only)
1 tablespoon minced cornichons
1 tablespoon Creole or whole-grain mustard
1 tablespoon ketchup
1½ teaspoons minced capers
Several dashes of hot sauce
Kosher salt and freshly ground black pepper

Burgers

2 tablespoons unsalted butter, at room temperature
4 potato hamburger buns, split
1½ pounds / 680g ground beef (80 percent lean and 20 percent fat), preferably certified Angus beef
¼ cup / 60ml canola oil, divided
8 slices American cheese
4 beefsteak tomato slices
4 green leaf lettuce leaves

1. Make the Cajun seasoning: In a small bowl, stir together the smoked paprika, granulated garlic, granulated onion, thyme, oregano, cayenne pepper, salt, and black pepper. Set aside.

2. Make the rémoulade: In a medium bowl, stir together the granulated garlic, mayonnaise, parsley, scallions, cornichons, mustard, ketchup, capers, and hot sauce. Season with salt and pepper and set aside.

3. Make the burgers: Place a wire rack on top of a baking sheet and set aside.

4. Heat a large cast-iron skillet over medium heat. Spread the butter evenly onto the cut sides of each of the buns. In batches, toast the buns cut-side down in the hot skillet until lightly crisped and browned in spots, about 1 minute. Transfer to a large plate and set aside. Increase the heat to medium-high.

5. Loosely form the ground beef into eight equal balls. Season two of the beef balls with a quarter of the Cajun seasoning (not all of the seasoning will stick to the beef, and that is okay as long as they are heavily coated). Add 1 tablespoon of the canola oil to the hot skillet and swirl the pan to coat. Add the two seasoned beef balls. Press down on one of the balls firmly with a large flat metal spatula for exactly 10 seconds (it should form a roughly ¼-inch / 6mm-thick beef patty), then gently remove the spatula and repeat with the second ball. Cook

RECIPE CONTINUES >>>

"A SMILE LOOKS GOOD ON YOU. YOU KNOW, SMILE?"

BENNY

until the patties are deeply browned and crusty on the first side, about 2 minutes. Flip the patties and top each with one slice of American cheese. Continue cooking until the cheese is melted around the edges and the second side of the patty is browned, about 1 additional minute. Transfer the cheesy beef patties to the wire rack and cover with foil to keep warm. Carefully pour out any excess oil and fat in the skillet and scrape out any cheese that is stuck to the bottom. Add fresh oil and repeat the prep and cooking process with the remaining meat, Cajun seasoning, and cheese, cleaning out and adding fresh oil to the skillet in between each batch.

6. Spread some of the rémoulade on the bottom buns and top each with two cheesy beef patties, a tomato slice, and a lettuce leaf. Top with additional rémoulade and the top buns and serve immediately.

Benny's French Fries

MAKES ABOUT 6 CUPS (ABOUT 1½ POUNDS / 680G)

2½ pounds / 1.1kg large russet potatoes
   (about 3 total)
Peanut or other vegetable oil, for frying
Kosher salt

1. Fill a large bowl with icy cold water and set aside. Peel the potatoes and cut lengthwise into ⅜-inch / 1cm-thick strips (between ¼ and ½ inch / 6mm and 1.3cm). As you cut the potatoes, place the strips into the ice water. After all of the potatoes have been cut, use your hands to swish the potatoes around several times to help release some of their starch, then drain the water. Fill the bowl of potatoes with fresh icy cold water and repeat this step two or three additional times, until the water runs clear. Drain the potatoes once more, fill with fresh icy cold water, wipe the outside of the bowl so that it's dry, cover it, and chill in the refrigerator for at least 2 and up to 8 hours.

2. When you are ready to fry, pour enough oil into a large Dutch oven to reach halfway up the sides and warm over medium-high heat until it reaches 325°F / 165°C on a deep-fry thermometer.

3. Meanwhile, drain the potatoes and run them several times through a salad spinner to remove as much water as possible. Spread the dried potato strips out onto a couple of baking sheets lined with clean kitchen towels or a couple layers of paper towels to aid in drying them even further. Use another clean towel or paper towels to lightly press any remaining moisture out of the potatoes. These steps are very important, as this will keep the fryer oil from splattering. Once completely dry, transfer the potato strips to a large bowl, then place two wire racks onto the baking sheets.

4. In batches, fry the potatoes until they are tender but still pale in color, stirring occasionally, about 3 minutes. The oil temperature will drop to around 300°F / 150°C, and that is okay. Use a slotted spoon or spider to transfer the par-fried potatoes to one of the wire racks; they can be slightly stacked if needed. Allow the oil to come back to temperature, then par-fry the remaining potatoes.

5. Once all of the potato strips have been par-fried, let the oil temperature rise to 370°F / 188°C. In batches, fry the par-fried potatoes until golden brown and crispy, stirring occasionally, about 3 additional minutes. The oil temperature will drop to around 350°F / 175°C, and that is okay. Transfer the twice-fried fries to the second wire rack and immediately season liberally with salt. Allow the oil to come back to temperature, then fry the remaining par-fried potatoes. Serve the hot fries immediately with the dipping sauce of your choice.

A Tuna Melt with Mustard, Dammit

Benny and Hop have known each other ever since Hop arrived in Hawkins. Hop, like most everyone, is a regular at Benny's Burgers. So much so that he's got his own special, a tuna melt with mustard and potato chips. Usually Benny remembers, but sometimes he doesn't. And when he doesn't, Hop lets him know.

SERVES 1

1 (5-ounce / 140g) can oil-packed tuna, drained well

¼ cup / 60g mayonnaise, plus 4 teaspoons, divided

Kosher salt and freshly ground black pepper

2 slices country-style white sandwich bread

1 tablespoon yellow mustard, plus more for topping

1 slice American cheese or cheddar cheese

½ cup / 20g potato chips

Dill pickle spears, for serving

1. Preheat the oven to 350°F / 175°C.

2. In a medium bowl, combine the tuna and ¼ cup / 60g of the mayonnaise, season with salt and pepper. Use a fork to smash down on the tuna and mix aggressively into the mayonnaise until the mixture is mostly smooth.

3. Heat a large cast-iron skillet over medium heat. Spread one of the bread slices with the mustard, then turn it over and spread the second side with 2 teaspoons of the remaining mayonnaise. Place the bread mayonnaise-side down in the hot skillet. Spoon the tuna mixture onto the bread and then top with the cheese.

4. Spread the remaining 2 teaspoons mayonnaise on the second slice of bread. Place the bread mayonnaise-side down next to the first slice of bread. Cook until the bread slices are lightly browned and crispy in spots (the bread will brown more in the oven), 3 to 4 minutes.

5. Transfer the skillet to the oven and bake until the cheese is completely melted, 3 to 5 minutes. Sprinkle the potato chips on the cheese and then squirt additional mustard over the chips. Top with the second slice of bread, transfer the sandwich to a cutting board, and cut in half.

6. Eat immediately with dill pickles straight from the jar.

Guest Check

Date	Table	Guests	Server	
				051197

APPT - SOUP/SAL - ENTREE - VEG/POT - DESSERT - BEV

1 Tuna Melt   —5

- ADD MUSTARD.
- ADD POTATO CHIPS
(ON SANDWICH)

Benny,
A tuna melt should
have mustard on it.
Dammit. And potato
chips. Jesus H. Christ.

Hop

| | Tax | |
| | Total | |

Guest Receipt

Date	Amount	Guests	Server	
				051197

MEMORIES

Jonathan,

I have to work late. Can you
PLEASE make dinner for Will.
These French Bread Pizzas are
one of his favorites and super
easy to make, I promise.

OK, love you.

Mom

Will's Favorite French Bread Pizza

SERVES 4

Though Joyce is a devoted mother, the Byers kids often fend for themselves. That means dinner must be something that even a child can make. Thankfully, it's also something that a child loves. One favorite is French Bread Pizza with a homemade tomato sauce. (But if you're not feeling that, a can of your favorite will do just fine too.)

2 tablespoons extra-virgin olive oil

2 garlic cloves, minced

1 (15-ounce / 425g) can crushed tomatoes

¼ teaspoon granulated sugar

½ teaspoon dried oregano, plus more for topping

Pinch of crushed red pepper flakes, plus more for topping

Kosher salt

1 (20-inch / 50cm-long) loaf French bread

3 tablespoons unsalted butter, melted

½ teaspoon granulated garlic, plus more for topping

3 cups / 336g shredded whole-milk, low-moisture mozzarella cheese, divided

2 tablespoons grated Parmesan cheese

1. In a small saucepan over medium heat, combine the olive oil and garlic. Cook, stirring constantly, until the garlic is softened, 1 to 2 minutes. Add the tomatoes, sugar, oregano, red pepper flakes, and a big pinch of salt. Bring to a simmer and cook, stirring occasionally, until most of the excess tomato juice has evaporated and the sauce has thickened, about 15 minutes. Remove from the heat and set aside.

2. Preheat the oven to 425°F / 220°C. Line a large baking sheet with parchment paper.

3. Cut the French loaf in half crosswise and then slice each piece in half lengthwise through the center, creating four equal "crusts" for the pizzas. Place the bread on the prepared baking sheet, brush the cut sides of the bread with the melted butter, and sprinkle with salt and the granulated garlic. Bake until the top and crust of the bread slices are barely toasted but the centers are still pillowy soft, about 3 minutes. Sprinkle with 1 cup / 112g of the mozzarella, then spoon on the sauce evenly, spreading it out to cover most of the cheese. Top with the remaining 2 cups / 224g mozzarella, then sprinkle evenly with the Parmesan.

4. Bake until the bread is crispy with browned edges and the cheese is completely melted, rotating the baking sheet 180 degrees after 5 minutes, for a total of 10 to 12 minutes.

5. Serve the pizzas immediately with additional oregano, red pepper flakes, and granulated garlic for topping.

COOK'S NOTE

For an Indiana special, try topping the pizzas with chopped crispy bacon, cooked crumbled Italian sausage, diced onions, and sauerkraut before popping them in the oven. Make sure to drain the sauerkraut really well so it doesn't make the bread soggy.

If you prefer your cheese more browned, you can broil the baked pizzas for a minute or two, but just make sure to watch them carefully so they don't burn.

Will's
Favorite
French Bread
Pizza
PAGE 43

"DO YOU WANNA BE NORMAL? DO YOU WANNA BE JUST
LIKE EVERYONE ELSE? BEING A FREAK IS THE BEST. I'M A FREAK!"

JONATHAN BYERS

Chinese Noodle Casserole

SERVES 8 TO 12

What could be more comforting than a casserole? Nothing, which is precisely why Karen drops one off for Joyce after Will goes missing. She even took the time to make this one—which is normally made just with canned soup—from scratch. The creamy sauce and the crunch of the crispy fried noodles offer exactly the type of support and care the Byers need as they search for Will.

¼ cup / 60ml canola oil, divided

12 ounces / 340g ground pork

Kosher salt and freshly ground black pepper

6 ounces / 170g shiitake mushrooms, stems removed and thinly sliced

1 yellow onion, coarsely chopped

4 garlic cloves, minced

1 red bell pepper, coarsely chopped

2 celery stalks, finely chopped

¼ cup / 35g all-purpose flour

2 cups / 475ml low-sodium chicken stock

1 cup / 240ml milk

¼ cup / 60ml soy sauce

⅔ cup / 130g jasmine rice, rinsed well

1 (8-ounce / 227g) can sliced water chestnuts, drained, rinsed, and coarsely chopped

1 cup / 130g frozen peas

2½ cups / 140g crispy chow mein noodles

Sliced scallions (green parts only), for topping

1. Preheat the oven to 350°F / 175°C. Lightly oil a 9 by 13-inch / 24 by 36cm baking dish and set aside.

2. In a large pot or Dutch oven over medium-high heat, warm 2 tablespoons of the canola oil until it starts to shimmer. Add the ground pork, season with salt and pepper, and cook, using a wooden spoon to break up the meat, until browned in spots and cooked through, 6 to 8 minutes.

3. Add 1 tablespoon of the remaining oil, the shiitake mushrooms, and onion, season with salt and pepper, and cook, stirring occasionally, until the vegetables are tender and browned in spots, 6 to 8 minutes. Stir in a splash of water if the bottom of the pot is getting too browned. Add the garlic, red bell pepper, celery, and a splash of water and cook, stirring constantly, for 2 minutes. Lower the heat to medium, stir in the remaining 1 tablespoon oil, then sprinkle the flour over the vegetables. Cook, stirring constantly, for 2 minutes. Slowly pour in the chicken stock and milk, stirring constantly, until there are no lumps of flour left. Add the soy sauce and bring the mixture to a simmer, stirring occasionally. Simmer until the mixture is thickened and similar to the consistency of thin gravy, about 5 minutes. Turn off the heat and season with additional salt and pepper if needed. Stir in the rice and water chestnuts and spoon the mixture into the prepared baking dish.

4. Tightly wrap the top of the baking dish with aluminum foil and bake until the rice is tender, about 30 minutes. Remove the baking dish from the oven, remove the foil, and stir in the peas. Sprinkle the top with the chow mein noodles. Bake uncovered until the sides of the casserole are bubbling and the peas and noodles are hot throughout, about 15 minutes.

5. Sprinkle the top of the casserole with sliced scallions and serve immediately.

COOK'S NOTE

To make this ahead of time to be enjoyed later, bake the casserole up to the point where you stir in the frozen peas, then let cool completely. Cover the baking dish and store in the refrigerator for up to 3 days. When you are ready to serve, uncover and reheat the casserole in an oven at 350°F / 175°C for 15 minutes. Remove from the oven, sprinkle with the chow mein noodles, and continue to cook until the casserole and the noodles are hot throughout, about 15 minutes.

Chicken à la King

SERVES 4 TO 6

Karen Wheeler is blessed with a love of cooking, the time for it, and a large, well-appointed kitchen. From there, she turns out dinners that would make Betty Crocker proud. Among her go-to recipes is this satisfying dish, popular since the mid-twentieth century in kitchens across America, made with chicken, cream, wine, mushrooms, and vegetables. Each element builds the flavor into a surprisingly complex dish, with no complicated technique needed.

12 frozen puff pastry shells, thawed

1 egg

Kosher salt and freshly ground black pepper

1 large bone-in, skin-on chicken breast
(about 12 ounces / 340g)

1½ teaspoons canola oil, plus 1 tablespoon,
divided

3 tablespoons unsalted butter, divided

8 ounces / 225g cremini mushrooms, sliced
⅛ inch / 3mm thick

2 large shallots, finely diced

1 small yellow bell pepper, coarsely chopped

2 celery stalks, coarsely chopped

½ cup / 120ml dry white wine

¼ cup / 35g all-purpose flour

2 cups / 475ml low-sodium chicken stock

½ cup / 120ml heavy cream

1 cup / 125g frozen peas and carrots

3 tablespoons diced sweet pimientos,
drained well

COOK'S NOTE

If you don't want to roast your own chicken, you can use 1½ cups / 225g of diced store-bought rotisserie chicken or any leftover cooked chicken you have on hand.

1. Position two racks in the upper and lower center of the oven and preheat to 425°F / 220°C. Line a large baking sheet with parchment paper and arrange the thawed pastry shells on the baking sheet.

2. In a small bowl, whisk together the egg and a splash of water. Brush the egg wash on the pastry shells and sprinkle the tops of the shells with salt and pepper.

3. Put the chicken breast onto a small baking sheet. Rub all over with 1½ teaspoons of the canola oil and season liberally with salt and pepper. Place both the pastry shells and the chicken into the oven. Bake the pastry shells until they puff and become deep golden brown, about 20 minutes. Roast the chicken until the skin is crisp and golden and a thermometer inserted into the thickest part of the breast registers 165°F / 75°C, 25 to 30 minutes. After the chicken is finished cooking, turn off the oven.

4. Once the pastry shells have cooled slightly, use a small knife to cut out the tops and soft inner layers so that the pastry shells are hollow. Trim away any of the excess pastry that is connected to the tops and place the trimmed tops and the hollowed-out shells back onto the baking sheet (you can save any excess pastry for a snack). Return the pastry shells to the oven that is now turned off. The residual heat from the oven will keep the shells warm while you make the filling.

5. When the chicken is cool enough to handle, remove the skin and bones and dice the meat into bite-size pieces (about 1½ cups / 225g). Set aside.

RECIPE CONTINUES >>>

6. In a large high-sided skillet over medium-high heat, warm the remaining 1 tablespoon oil and 1 tablespoon of the butter. Once the butter has melted, add the mushrooms and cook, stirring occasionally, until tender and browned in spots, 8 to 10 minutes. Lower the heat to medium, add the remaining 2 tablespoons butter and the shallots, season with salt and pepper, and cook, stirring frequently, until tender, about 5 minutes. Add the yellow bell pepper and celery and cook, stirring frequently, until crisp-tender, 3 to 4 minutes. Stir in the wine, scrape up any browned bits at the bottom of the skillet, and cook, stirring constantly, for 2 minutes. Sprinkle the flour over the vegetables and cook, stirring constantly, for 2 minutes. Slowly pour in the chicken stock and heavy cream, stirring constantly, until there are no lumps of flour left.

Continue to whisk until the mixture comes to a simmer. Cook, stirring occasionally, until the mixture is thickened and looks similar to a rich and creamy gravy, about 10 minutes. Stir in the cooked chicken, frozen peas and carrots, and pimientos. Bring back to a simmer and cook, stirring occasionally, until the chicken, peas, and carrots are hot throughout, 3 to 5 minutes. Season with salt and pepper.

7. Divide the warm pastry shells among four to six serving plates and spoon the filling into the center of each shell, overfilling the shells so that some of the filling spills over the sides. Top the filling in each shell with one of the pastry tops and serve immediately.

Christmas Lasagna

SERVES 8 TO 12

*Some very odd events might be happening at
the Byers House off Mirkwood. Will's missing
and the Christmas lights speak to Joyce. They
are not, as she says herself, a "normal family."
But that doesn't mean they don't enjoy a good
old-fashioned sit-down dinner when they get the
chance. This lasagna is filling, delicious, easy
to make, easier to save, and affordable. It's
convenient enough for a weeknight meal and
special enough for a holiday. Plus it keeps well
frozen, for whenever Will surfaces.*

4 cups / 910g 4% milk fat small-curd cottage
    cheese

2 tablespoons extra-virgin olive oil

1½ pounds / 680g bulk mild or hot Italian sausage
    (no casings)

1 yellow onion, coarsely chopped

4 garlic cloves, minced

1 (6-ounce / 170g) can tomato paste

⅔ cup / 160ml dry red wine

1 (28-ounce / 794g) can crushed tomatoes

1 (14.5-ounce / 411g) can petite diced tomatoes,
    drained

1½ teaspoons Italian seasoning

Kosher salt and freshly ground black pepper

2 eggs

6 cups / 690g shredded whole-milk, low-moisture
    mozzarella cheese, divided

1 cup / 100g grated Parmesan cheese, divided

9 lasagna noodles, uncooked

1. Set a large wire-mesh strainer over a medium
bowl. Spoon the cottage cheese into the strainer,
then lay a small plate directly onto the cheese and
place a heavy can on top of the plate. Allow the
excess liquid to drain from the cottage cheese.

2. In a large pot over medium-high heat, warm
the olive oil until it just starts to shimmer. Add
the sausage and cook, using a wooden spoon to
break up the meat, until browned in spots,
8 to 10 minutes. Add the onion and cook, stirring
occasionally, until tender, 6 to 8 minutes. Then
add the garlic and cook, stirring constantly, until
softened, 1 to 2 minutes. Add the tomato paste
and cook, stirring constantly, for 2 minutes. Add
the red wine and cook, stirring constantly, for
2 minutes more.

3. Add the crushed tomatoes, diced tomatoes, and
Italian seasoning to the pot. Season with salt and
pepper, stir to combine, and bring to a simmer.
Cook, partially covered, stirring occasionally, for
30 minutes. The sauce will not look very different
at this point, but the flavors will have had time to
marry. Season with additional salt and pepper, if
needed. Remove from the heat and set aside.

4. In a medium bowl, whisk the eggs until smooth.
Add the drained cottage cheese (discard the excess
liquid), 1½ cups / 173g of the mozzarella, and
¼ cup / 25g of the Parmesan; season with salt
and pepper and stir together until well combined.
Set aside.

RECIPE
CONTINUES >>>

5. Preheat the oven to 375°F / 190°C. Lightly oil a 9 by 13-inch / 24 by 36cm baking dish. Spread 2 cups / 475ml of the meat sauce on the bottom of the prepared baking dish. Lay three of the lasagna noodles on top of the sauce, spacing them evenly since they will expand as they cook. Spread half of the cottage cheese mixture over the noodles. Sprinkle with 1½ cups / 173g of the remaining mozzarella and ¼ cup / 25g of the Parmesan. Spread 2 cups of the meat sauce on top of the cheese. Layer with another three noodles, the remaining cottage cheese, 1½ cups / 173g mozzarella, and ¼ cup / 25g Parmesan. Layer one last time with 2 cups / 475ml of the meat sauce, three noodles, and the remaining sauce. Tightly wrap the top of the lasagna with aluminum foil and place onto a large rimmed baking sheet.

6. Bake the lasagna for 40 minutes and then remove from the oven. Remove the foil and top with the remaining mozzarella and Parmesan. Return to the oven and continue to bake until the cheese is browned in spots and a wooden skewer inserted into the center of the lasagna goes through without any resistance (this means that the noodles are fully cooked), about 30 minutes more. Allow to rest for 20 minutes.

7. When ready to serve, slice into individual portions.

Fennel Salad with Raspberry Vinaigrette

SERVES 4

Raspberry vinaigrette was the dressing du jour of the 1980s. It came first from the nouvelle cuisine movement in France in which chefs lightened and reinvented traditional French recipes with more produce, less cream, and a market-driven approach. That seeped into the consciousness of California cooks like Alice Waters and Wolfgang Puck. Soon enough, raspberry vinaigrette arrived in bottles, to coat the lettuces and greens of Americans across the country.

1 cup / 120g raspberries, divided

⅓ cup / 80ml extra-virgin olive oil, plus 1 tablespoon, divided

¼ cup / 60ml white wine vinegar

2 to 4 teaspoons honey (depending on the sweetness of the raspberries)

1½ teaspoons Dijon mustard

Kosher salt and freshly ground black pepper

½ red onion

2 bulbs fennel

1 ruby red grapefruit

1 avocado

COOK'S NOTE If you have any leftover vinaigrette, transfer it to an airtight container and store in the refrigerator for up to 5 days.

1. In a blender, combine half of the raspberries, ⅓ cup / 80ml of the olive oil, the vinegar, honey, and mustard. Season with salt and pepper and blend until very smooth. Set the vinaigrette aside.

2. Very thinly slice the onion and transfer to a large bowl. Cut away and discard the tops of the fennel but reserve a small handful of the fronds. Cut the bulbs in half crosswise, remove and discard the core, and cut into very thin slices. (You want it to be almost shaved; you can use a mandoline to make this task even easier.) Add the fennel slices to the onion. Set aside.

3. Slice the top and bottom off the grapefruit and sit it flat on a cutting board. Slice along the curve of the fruit from the top to the bottom to remove the peel and pith. Working over a bowl to catch any juices, use a small paring knife to cut between the membrane of the fruit to yield the segments. Squeeze any remaining juice from the fruit into the bowl and set the segments and juice aside. Slice the avocado in half, remove the pit, and thinly slice the flesh. Spoon a bit of the grapefruit juice over the avocado slices, which will help prevent browning.

4. Drizzle 2 tablespoons of the grapefruit juice and the remaining 1 tablespoon oil over the fennel and onion, season with salt and pepper, and gently toss to combine. Transfer half of the mixture to a large serving platter and nestle half of the grapefruit segments and half of the avocado slices into the fennel. Drizzle with a couple spoonfuls of the raspberry vinaigrette. Top with the remaining fennel and onion and nestle the remaining grapefruit, avocado, and raspberries into the fennel. Drizzle with additional vinaigrette and garnish with the fennel fronds.

5. Serve the salad immediately with any remaining vinaigrette on the side.

Hawkins Middle School Chocolate Pudding

SERVES 4 TO 6

The original name for chocolate mousse was mayonnaise de chocolat. *But when Betty Crocker introduced it to America in 1950 (using chocolate syrup), its name had changed to mousse. This version—lighter than regular pudding but more dense than a mousse—honors the original name with the addition of mayonnaise, which gives the pudding a rich, creamy texture.*

¾ cup / 150g packed light brown sugar
⅓ cup / 25g natural unsweetened cocoa powder
3 tablespoons cornstarch
2¾ cups / 650ml milk
½ cup / 120g mayonnaise
2 teaspoons vanilla extract

1. Set a fine-mesh strainer over a medium saucepan. Add the brown sugar, cocoa powder, and cornstarch to the strainer and use the back of a rubber spatula to stir and push the dry ingredients through the strainer and into the saucepan. (Or use a flour sifter if you have one.)

2. Remove the strainer and slowly whisk the milk into the dry ingredients until smooth and the mixture resembles chocolate milk. Add the mayonnaise and whisk again until smooth. Bring to a simmer over medium heat, 6 to 8 minutes. Once at a simmer, cook, whisking constantly, until the mixture has thickened to the consistency of pudding, about 2 minutes more.

3. Remove from the heat and whisk in the vanilla. Immediately place a piece of plastic wrap directly on top of the pudding. Let cool at room temperature for 30 minutes and then refrigerate until completely chilled, at least 3 hours or up to overnight.

4. When ready to serve, whisk the chilled pudding vigorously until it is smooth and creamy and then divide evenly among four to six glass jars or small cups.

"MIKE, I FOUND THE CHOCOLATE PUDDING!"

DUSTIN

HAWKINS
MIDDLE SCHOOL

A.V. CLUB

A YEAR AFTER the Mothergate was torn open in a sub-basement of the National Laboratory, Hawkins is still trying to return to normal. Whatever that means. Mike, Will, Dustin, and Lucas have returned to the realms of Mirkwood, D&D campaigns, to friendship, to snacks. But new families (new creatures, new threats) have arrived too. Handsome but dangerous Billy Hargrove, with his flowing sun-kissed locks and well-formed biceps, lands in Hawkins like a cannonball in the community pool, with his skateboarding stepsister, Max Mayfield, in tow. As Will tries to put the past behind him, Mike searches for Eleven, and Eleven searches for Mike. New love lurks too. Joyce and her new boyfriend, Bob, best known from Radio Shack, find each other. Lucas and Max flirt. Nancy likes Steve, Jonathan likes Nancy, and eventually Nancy and Jonathan like each other. In the midst of their teenage years, everyone is pursuing their own story. As it should be.

But when the Mind Flayer entwines its vines around Hawkins, the town is thrown into turmoil again. Even Hopper can't stop the Demodogs, or keep Eleven safely hidden in his cabin. Will is once again caught in the thrall of a powerful evil creature, and Joyce, Jonathan, Bob, and the rest of his friends race to save him. There seems to be no rest for the weary and no quarter for the faint of heart.

What unites each Hawkins resident is food. How does Hop lure Eleven out of her room? His famous Eggo Extravaganza. How does Bob prove he's there for the long run? His famous Speedway Chili. How do Nancy and Steve console Barb's grieving parents? Over plates of Baked Ziti. The year 1984 may have been the scariest, most terrifying one in Hawkins' history, but it also might be one of the most delicious.

RECIPES

El's Eggo Extravaganza

SERVES 4

Eleven can't resist a waffle, but can you blame her? Since 1953, Eggo frozen waffles have been a breakfast favorite, popping out of the toaster like the rising sun. Even better are these homemade versions, stacked into a decadent tower, with layers of whipped cream and candy. It's not breakfast, it's a totally over-the-top declaration of sweetness. And if you just want to use Eggo waffles, go ahead. No judgment.

1¼ cups / 175g all-purpose flour
⅓ cup / 45g cornstarch
¼ cup / 50g granulated sugar
2 teaspoons baking powder
½ teaspoon kosher salt
2 egg whites
2 tablespoons canola oil
1⅓ cups / 315ml milk
4 teaspoons vanilla extract, divided
2 tablespoons unsalted butter, melted
Cooking spray
3 cups / 720ml heavy cream, cold
½ cup / 60g confectioners' sugar
60 drop-shaped milk chocolate candies, such as Hershey's Kisses
¾ cup / 140g candy-coated peanut butter candies, such as Reese's Pieces
1 cup / 220g large jelly beans

Special Equipment
1 (4-inch / 10cm) waffle iron
1 large piping bag fitted with a large star tip

1. In a medium bowl, combine the flour, cornstarch, granulated sugar, baking powder, and salt and whisk until well combined. In another medium bowl, whisk the egg whites until light and frothy. Add the canola oil, milk, and 2 teaspoons of the vanilla and whisk until smooth, then whisk in the melted butter. Add the milk mixture to the flour mixture and whisk until just combined (do not overmix; some small lumps are okay). Let rest for 5 minutes.

2. Meanwhile, preheat a waffle iron according to the manufacturer's directions and lightly coat with cooking spray.

3. Add a scant ¼ cup / 60ml of the batter to the waffle iron, spreading the batter to cover most of the surface. Close the top and cook until the waffle is cooked through, browned, and crispy, 4 to 5 minutes. Remove from the iron and repeat the process with the remaining batter, about 12 waffles total. Set aside to cool while you make the whipped cream.

4. In a large bowl, combine the heavy cream, confectioners' sugar, and remaining 2 teaspoons vanilla. Use an electric handheld mixer to blend on low speed until the ingredients are incorporated, then whip on medium-high speed until medium-stiff peaks form. Transfer the whipped cream to a large piping bag fitted with a large star tip. (This might have to be done in two batches, depending on the size of the piping bag.)

5. In the center of a large plate, pipe a swirl of whipped cream that is the same size as a waffle. Place three chocolate candies into the whipped cream and then top with a cooled waffle. Layer the waffle with more whipped cream, another three chocolate candies, a second waffle, more whipped cream, three chocolate candies, a third waffle, whipped cream, three chocolate candies, 1 tablespoon peanut butter candies, and 2 tablespoons jelly beans. Scatter three chocolate candies, 2 tablespoons peanut butter candies, and 2 tablespoons jelly beans around the bottom of the waffle. Repeat this to make another three extravaganzas. Eat immediately.

"FRIENDS DON'T LIE."

ELEVEN

Erica Sinclair

Hypothesis #1: If my pancakes could have even 🡒
more maple syrup, then they would be delicious.

Fact #1: Putting maple syrup on a stack of pancakes
makes them soggy.

Fact #2: Putting maple syrup ~~e~~on pancakes means
- fighting with Lucas for the syrup.

Hypothesis #2: If maple syrup can be used during the
cooking of the pancakes, then the maple syrup flavor 🗙
will be stronger and the pancakes will be more delicious.

Experiment #1: I replaced the maple syrup for the sugar
in the buttermilk pancake batter. In addition,

Experiment #2: I added maple syrup to the butter used
on top of the pancakes.

Result: My ~~hypothesises~~ hypotheses were correct.
These maple syrup pancakes are even more delicious.

Double Maple Syrup Pancakes

MAKES 10 PANCAKES

Breakfast at the Sinclair residence is a scramble. Lucas and his sister, Erica, have both a healthy sibling rivalry and healthy appetites. The latter is no surprise, as Sue Sinclair has a special touch for the breakfast classics. One example is this decadent stack of pancakes, developed with Erica for a homework assignment on the scientific method.

Salted Maple Butter

½ cup / 110g unsalted butter, at room temperature
3 tablespoons pure maple syrup
½ teaspoon kosher salt

Maple Pancakes

1⅔ cups / 230g all-purpose flour
1½ teaspoons baking powder
¾ teaspoon baking soda
½ teaspoon kosher salt
1 egg
¼ cup / 60ml pure maple syrup, plus more for serving
1⅓ cups / 315ml buttermilk
3 tablespoons unsalted butter, melted and cooled slightly
2 tablespoons canola oil

1. **Make the salted maple butter:** In a small bowl, combine the butter, maple syrup, and salt. Stir to combine until smooth. Set aside.

2. **Make the maple pancakes:** In a large bowl, whisk together the flour, baking powder, baking soda, and salt. In a medium bowl, whisk together the egg, maple syrup, and buttermilk until smooth. Add the slightly cooled melted butter and whisk again until smooth. Pour the wet ingredients into the dry ingredients and whisk until just combined. The batter will be thick and a little lumpy, and that is okay; do not overmix. Rest the batter at room temperature for 10 minutes.

3. Preheat the oven to 200°F / 95°C.

4. After the batter has rested, heat a large nonstick skillet over medium heat. Lightly brush with some of the canola oil. Scoop ⅓ cup / 80ml of the batter into the skillet and use a small spoon to spread the batter out into a pancake that is about 4 inches / 10cm in diameter and ½ inch / 1.3cm thick. Repeat to add one or two more pancakes to the skillet (depending on the size of your skillet). Cook until the tops of the pancakes are covered in bubbles, the edges look set, and the undersides are nicely browned, 3 to 4 minutes. If the pancakes are browning too quickly, lower the heat to medium-low. Flip and continue cooking until lightly browned on the second side, about 2 additional minutes. Transfer to a large baking sheet and place in the oven to keep warm while you make the rest of the pancakes. Repeat with the remaining batter, brushing the skillet with more oil as needed, making about 10 pancakes total.

5. Serve the pancakes in short stacks topped with the salted maple butter and additional maple syrup.

Barb's Baked Ziti

SERVES 8 TO 10

Steve and Nancy know dinner at the Hollands is going to be heavy. After all, Barb's been missing for nearly a year and her parents are grieving. What they didn't expect is Marsha Holland hiring a private investigator named Murray Bauman, better known as a former journalist from Chicago, to look into Barb's death, or Marsha cooking one of Nancy's favorites from the Holland family repertoire: a Greek-inspired cinnamon-spiced baked ziti she used to love from her visits with Barb, back in better times.

2 tablespoons extra-virgin olive oil
1½ pounds / 680g ground lamb
Kosher salt and freshly ground black pepper
1 yellow onion, finely chopped
¼ cup / 65g tomato paste
4 garlic cloves, minced
2 teaspoons dried oregano
1½ teaspoons ground cinnamon
½ teaspoon crushed red pepper flakes
¾ cup / 175ml dry red wine
1 (28-ounce / 794g) can crushed tomatoes
1 pound / 450g ziti pasta
1 egg
⅓ cup / 80ml heavy cream
1½ pounds / 680g whole-milk ricotta cheese
½ cup / 50g grated Parmesan cheese
4 cups / 450g shredded whole-milk, low-moisture
    mozzarella cheese

COOK'S NOTE

When shopping for ricotta, make sure to get a good-quality, ultra-creamy one, which will help to better mimic the cheesy béchamel that usually tops pastitsio.

1. In a large pot over medium-high heat, warm the olive oil until it just starts to shimmer. Add the lamb, season with salt and pepper, and cook, using a wooden spoon to break up the meat, until browned in spots and cooked through, 8 to 10 minutes. Add the onion and cook, stirring occasionally, until tender, 6 to 8 minutes. Add the tomato paste, garlic, oregano, cinnamon, and red pepper flakes and cook, stirring constantly, for 2 minutes.

2. Stir in the wine, scrape up any browned bits at the bottom of the pot, and cook, stirring constantly, for 2 minutes. Add the crushed tomatoes, season with salt and pepper, and bring to a simmer. Cook, partially covered, until the sauce is slightly reduced and thickened, stirring occasionally, about 30 minutes. Remove from the heat and set aside.

3. Bring a large pot of salted water to a boil. Add the ziti and cook for 2 minutes less than the package directions for al dente doneness, about 8 minutes. Reserve ½ cup / 120ml of the pasta water, then drain the pasta well and rinse with cold water. Stir the reserved pasta water into the meat sauce and season with additional salt and pepper if needed. Add 2 cups / 475ml of the meat sauce to the cooked ziti, stir to combine, then set aside.

4. Preheat the oven to 375°F / 190°C. Lightly oil a 9 by 13-inch / 24 by 36cm baking dish and set aside.

5. In a medium bowl, combine the egg and heavy cream and whisk until smooth. Add the ricotta and ¼ cup / 25g of the Parmesan and whisk again until smooth. Season with salt and pepper and stir in 1 cup / 112g of the mozzarella.

6. Spread 1 cup / 240ml of the meat sauce on the bottom of the prepared baking dish. Top with half of the pasta and half of the remaining sauce, spoon large dollops of half of the ricotta mixture on top of the sauce, then sprinkle with half of the remaining mozzarella and Parmesan. Repeat this layering process once more.

7. Place the baking dish onto a baking sheet and bake until the cheese is browned in spots and the edges of the ziti are bubbling, about 30 minutes. Allow to rest for 10 minutes.

8. Scoop the ziti into individual portions and serve immediately.

A Steak
and a Potato

Jim Hopper is not a man of teaspoons and tablespoons. He's not a baker. He's not a chef. He's a meat-and-potatoes guy. His favorite recipes are, like him, gruff.

A STEAK AND A POTATO

- Buy steak.
- Scrub potato.
- Heat skillet plus oil.
- Heat oven hot.
- Cut potato into chunks.
- Sear potato.
- Kill a Schlitz.
- Add steak to skillet.
- Wait 3-5 minutes.
- Turn steak.
- Stir potatoes.
- Wait 3-4 minutes.
- Add butter to steak.
- Put in oven.
- Drink another beer.
- Take out steak.
- One more beer.
- Take skillet from oven.
- Eat everything all together.

Bob's Speedway Chili

SERVES 6 TO 8

If Bob Newby was a dish, he'd be something with heart, something comforting and warm. Makes sense, therefore, that his specialty is this chili, as Indiana a recipe as you'll find. When he left a crock of it for Joyce when she returned from work, she knew he was the one for her.

12 ounces / 340g Hatch green chiles (4 to 6 total; see Cook's Note)

2 tablespoons canola oil

1½ pounds / 680g lean ground turkey or beef

Kosher salt and freshly ground black pepper

1 yellow onion, coarsely chopped

3 garlic cloves, minced

¼ cup / 24g chili powder

2 teaspoons ground cumin

3 (15-ounce / 425g) cans diced fire-roasted tomatoes

2 cups / 475ml tomato juice

2 cups / 475ml beef stock

2 (15-ounce / 425g) cans chili beans (pinto or kidney beans in mild sauce)

Sour cream, for topping

Shredded sharp cheddar cheese, for sprinkling

1. Preheat a charcoal grill, gas grill, or cast-iron grill pan to medium-high heat.

2. Arrange the chiles on the grill in a single layer and cook until tender and deeply charred and blackened in spots, turning the chiles as needed to ensure even charring, 10 to 15 minutes. The timing for this will depend heavily on the heat of the grill you are using.

3. Transfer the chiles to a medium bowl, cover the top with plastic wrap, and let steam for 20 minutes. Remove the skin and seeds, then coarsely chop and set aside.

4. In a large Dutch oven or pot over medium-high heat, warm the canola oil until it starts to shimmer. Add the ground turkey or beef, season with salt and pepper, and cook until browned and cooked through, using a wooden spoon to break up the meat, 8 to 10 minutes. Add the onion, season with salt and pepper, and cook until softened, 8 to 10 minutes. Add the garlic, chili powder, and cumin and cook, stirring constantly, until the garlic is softened, about 2 minutes. Add the grilled and chopped Hatch green chiles, diced tomatoes, tomato juice, and beef stock. Stir to combine, taste for seasoning, and bring to a simmer. Cook, stirring occasionally, until slightly reduced and thickened, about 45 minutes.

5. Stir in the chili beans, bring back to a simmer, and cook, stirring occasionally, for an additional 30 minutes. Taste again for seasoning.

6. Scoop the chili into bowls, top with dollops of sour cream, and sprinkle with shredded cheddar.

COOK'S NOTE

Fresh Hatch green chiles are available only in fall, in and around New Mexico; if you can't get those, you can substitute with ¾ cup / 6 ounces / 170g of canned or frozen (and thawed) roasted and chopped Hatch green chiles instead. If you prefer using fresh chiles, Anaheim chiles are a great stand-in but are milder in flavor.

Some Hoosiers like to add pasta to their chili. To do so, stir a handful of dried elbow macaroni and a large splash of beef stock (or water) into the chili 15 minutes after you add the beans, and cook until the pasta is tender, about 15 minutes.

"IT'S GONNA BE OKAY. REMEMBER,
BOB NEWBY, SUPERHERO."

BOB

Deep-Dish Pumpkin Pie

SERVES 8 TO 10

Something is killing the pumpkins in Hawkins. Is it downy mildew? Is it feuding farmers Eugene McCorkle or Merrill Wright? Turns out it's neither. (It's the Upside Down!) Thankfully the season's favorite pumpkin pie had already been made by the time the patch was destroyed. Using the smaller sugar pumpkin—sweeter than the Halloween variety—this pie uses all the warming spices of autumn plus a dollop of cinnamon whipped cream.

1 sugar pumpkin (about 4 pounds / 1.8kg)

5 tablespoons / 75g unsalted butter, cubed

5 tablespoons / 62g vegetable shortening

1¾ cups / 245g all-purpose flour

1½ tablespoons granulated sugar

1½ teaspoons kosher salt, divided

¼ cup / 60ml to ⅓ cup / 80ml ice water

2 large eggs, at room temperature

1 large egg yolk, at room temperature

¾ cup / 150g packed dark brown sugar, plus 2 tablespoons

1½ teaspoons ground cinnamon, divided

1 tablespoon cornstarch, plus 1 teaspoon

½ teaspoon ground ginger

¼ teaspoon freshly grated nutmeg

⅛ teaspoon ground cloves

Pinch of freshly ground black pepper (optional)

1 cup / 240ml half-and-half or heavy cream, at room temperature

3 tablespoons confectioners' sugar

1 cup / 240ml heavy cream, cold

1. Preheat the oven to 425°F / 220°C. Line a baking sheet with parchment paper.

2. Lay the pumpkin on its side and, using a sharp knife, carefully cut away the side that has the stem. Sit the pumpkin upright and slice it in half vertically until you get to the sturdy bottom. Remove the knife from the pumpkin and use your hands to crack it in half. Using a spoon, remove the seeds from the center of the pumpkin and scrape out as much of the stringy innards as possible. Using your hands, liberally rub water all over the flesh side of the pumpkin and then place cut-side down on the prepared baking sheet. Roast, rotating the baking sheet 180 degrees after 30 minutes, until the pumpkin is very tender (you should be able to smash down on the flesh with the tines of a fork without any effort; you can also roast the seeds and eat them as a snack), about 1 hour. Remove from the oven and let cool completely. Turn the oven off for now.

3. While the pumpkin is roasting and cooling, put the cubed butter and vegetable shortening into the freezer for 20 minutes.

4. In a large bowl, combine the flour, granulated sugar, and 1 teaspoon of the salt. Add the cold butter and vegetable shortening and use a pastry cutter or your fingertips to cut the butter and shortening into the flour until the texture resembles coarse meal. Drizzle ¼ cup / 60ml of the ice water over the flour mixture and use your hands to mix until the dough just starts to come together, adding more water, 1 teaspoon at a time, if needed.

5. Transfer the dough onto a large piece of plastic wrap, press mostly smooth, and flatten into a 1-inch / 2.5cm-thick disk. Wrap tightly and let chill in the refrigerator for 1 hour.

COOK'S NOTE

If you don't want to make fresh pumpkin puree, use 1 (15-ounce / 425g) can of store-bought pure pumpkin puree instead. Because canned pumpkin is a touch drier, decrease the cornstarch to 1 tablespoon.

6. On a lightly floured work surface, roll the dough into a 14-inch / 36cm round that is a little bit thinner than ⅛ inch / 3mm. Carefully roll the dough around the rolling pin and then unroll into a 9-inch / 24cm deep-dish pie plate. Gently press the dough into the pie plate and trim the edges, leaving 1 inch / 2.5cm of overhang. Fold the overhanging dough under itself and crimp the edges with your fingers. Pierce the bottom all over with a fork. Refrigerate the crust until it is firm, about 30 minutes.

7. Put a baking sheet onto the lowest oven rack and preheat to 375°F / 190°C.

8. Line the chilled crust with parchment paper or aluminum foil and fill with dry rice or beans or baking weights.

9. Bake the crust on the hot baking sheet until the edges of the dough begin to feel dry and set and start to brown, about 20 minutes. Carefully remove the parchment paper or foil and the rice, beans, or weights. Return to the oven and continue to bake until the edges and bottom of the crust are lightly browned and cooked through, about 15 minutes more. Remove from the oven and let cool slightly while you make the filling (leave the oven on and the baking sheet in the oven).

10. Scoop the flesh of the pumpkin out of the skin and into a food processor and process until very smooth. Measure out 1¾ cups / 415g and place in a large bowl. (Reserve the remaining puree for another use.) Add the eggs and yolk and brown sugar and whisk until smooth. Add 1 teaspoon of the cinnamon, the cornstarch, ginger, nutmeg, cloves, the remaining ½ teaspoon salt, the black pepper (if using), and half-and-half and whisk vigorously until well combined and smooth. Pour into the warm crust.

11. Bake on the hot baking sheet, rotating the baking sheet 180 degrees after 30 minutes, until the edges of the filling are set but the center is still a touch jiggly (it will set up fully once cooled), 50 minutes to 1 hour. If the edges of the crust start to get too brown before the filling is finished cooking, cover them with aluminum foil or a pie crust shield. Remove from the oven and let cool completely on the baking sheet, 3 to 4 hours.

12. Just before serving, in a medium bowl, combine the remaining ½ teaspoon cinnamon, the confectioners' sugar, and heavy cream. Use a handheld mixer to blend on low speed until the ingredients are incorporated, then whip on medium-high speed until medium-stiff peaks form.

13. To serve, slice the pie into 8 to 10 wedges and top with dollops of the cinnamon whipped cream.

Hawkins PD's Trick-or-Treat Sugar Cocoa Cookies

MAKES 16 COOKIES

God bless Flo, who keeps the phones answered, the coffee hot, and the donuts baked. Come Halloween, she makes these police-themed badge-shaped sugar cocoa cookies for trick-or-treaters brave enough to knock on the Hawkins PD front door. That is, if she can keep them hidden from Officer Powell and Officer Callahan. For two cops, they're expert cookie thieves.

1⅔ cups / 230g all-purpose flour, plus more for dusting

2 tablespoons unsweetened cocoa powder

½ teaspoon baking powder

¼ teaspoon kosher salt

1½ teaspoons instant coffee granules

1 tablespoon vanilla extract, divided

6 tablespoons / 85g unsalted butter, at room temperature

⅔ cup / 130g granulated sugar

1 egg

1 pound / 450g (about 3½ cups) confectioners' sugar

2 tablespoons meringue powder

⅓ cup / 80ml water, plus more if needed

Gold gel food coloring

Gold candy sequins or other decorative round gold sprinkles or candies, for decorating

Royal blue gel food coloring

Special Equipment

1 (3½-inch / 8.8cm) sheriff star cookie cutter

2 piping bags fitted with 1/16-inch / 2mm-round piping tips

1. Preheat the oven to 350°F / 175°C. Line two baking sheets with parchment paper.

2. In a medium bowl, whisk together the flour, cocoa powder, baking powder, and salt. Set aside.

3. In a large bowl, whisk together the coffee granules and half of the vanilla extract until the coffee granules are completely dissolved. Add the butter and granulated sugar and use a handheld mixer to blend on low speed to incorporate the sugar into the butter. Turn the speed to medium-high and blend until the mixture is well combined, scraping down the bowl as needed. Add the egg and blend until smooth and creamy. Add half of the flour mixture and blend until almost combined. Add the remaining flour and blend until the mixture is well combined and crumbly. Use your hands to mix the dough until it comes together to form a smooth ball.

4. Lightly dust a work surface with flour and set out the cookie dough. Divide the dough in two, cover half with a kitchen towel or plastic wrap, and set aside. Roll the remaining half of the dough out into a ¼-inch / 6mm-thick round. Use a sheriff star cookie cutter to cut out eight cookies, rerolling the scraps as needed. Arrange the cookies on one of the prepared baking sheets.

5. Bake, rotating the baking sheet 180 degrees halfway through, until the tops of the cookies are dry and have gone from shiny to matte, about 10 minutes. Let cool for 5 minutes on the baking sheet, then transfer to a wire rack to cool completely.

6. As the first batch of cookies are cooling, roll and cut out the remaining dough into eight additional cookies and arrange on the second baking sheet. Repeat the baking and cooling process once more.

7. While the cookies are cooling, fit two pastry bags with small round tips and set aside. In a large bowl, combine the confectioners' sugar, meringue powder, the remaining vanilla extract, and water

RECIPE CONTINUES »»»

and beat with a handheld mixer on medium-high speed until the icing forms thick and glossy peaks. Add additional water, ½ teaspoon at a time, if needed to achieve a thick but pipeable consistency. Scoop out 1 cup / 240ml of the white royal icing and reserve it in a small bowl.

8. To the large bowl of royal icing, stir in drops of gold gel food coloring until the icing is a deep golden color. Transfer half of the gold icing to one of the prepared piping bags. Cover the bowl with the remaining gold icing with plastic wrap and set aside. Pipe the gold royal icing around the outer edge of one of the cooled cookies. Working quickly before the icing dries, place a gold sequin on each of the rounded tips of the sheriff star. Pipe the edges of the remaining cookies and top with more sequins. Allow the icing to set completely, about 30 minutes.

9. Squeeze out any of the excess icing from the piping bag back into the bowl with the remaining gold icing. Stir until the gold icing is well combined and smooth. Thin the icing with water, ½ teaspoon at a time, until it is the consistency of maple syrup (thick but fluid). Scoop the thinned-out gold icing into the second prepared pastry bag.

10. Fill the inside of one of the cookies with the thinner gold icing and use a wooden skewer to help spread the icing to the corners of the cookie. Repeat until all of the cookies are iced. Allow the icing to set completely, about 2 hours.

11. Clean and dry one of the piping bags and tips. To the small bowl of reserved white icing, stir in drops of royal blue gel food coloring until the icing is a deep blue color. Transfer the blue icing to the clean and dry piping bag and pipe the names of your favorite Hawkins police officers onto the sheriff star cookies. Allow the icing to set completely before serving, about 1 hour.

12. Serve the cookies the day they are made or transfer them to an airtight container and store at room temperature for up to 5 days.

Steve Harrington's No-Fail Crêpes Suzette

SERVES 2

As Steve Harrington knows, any budding Casanova needs a signature recipe. Ideally, it's something easy to make but with a bit of spectacle. It should be sweet. It should be quick. It should not be easy to mess up. Steve's recipe is a crêpes Suzette, and it has worked well for him.

2 tablespoons sour cream, plus more for serving
½ cup / 120ml whole milk
1 egg
1 tablespoon granulated sugar
1 teaspoon vanilla extract
½ cup / 70g all-purpose flour
¼ teaspoon kosher salt
1 tablespoon unsalted butter, melted
Canola oil, for the skillet

½ cup / 155g orange marmalade
⅓ cup / 80ml fresh orange juice
3 tablespoons orange liqueur, such as Grand Marnier or Cointreau
3 tablespoons cold unsalted butter, cut into ½-inch / 1.3cm cubes
Confectioners' sugar, for topping

Special Equipment
1 (10-inch / 25cm) nonstick skillet or crêpe pan

1. In a medium bowl, combine the sour cream, milk, egg, granulated sugar, and vanilla. Whisk until smooth. Add the flour and salt and whisk vigorously until the batter is smooth and creamy. Add the melted butter and whisk again until well combined. Cover the bowl with plastic wrap and let the batter rest at room temperature for 30 minutes.

2. After the batter has rested, whisk it again to ensure the batter is well blended. Heat a 10-inch / 25cm nonstick skillet or crêpe pan over medium to medium-high heat. Dab some canola oil onto a paper towel and wipe a very thin layer of oil onto the skillet.

RECIPE CONTINUES >>>

3. Remove the skillet from the heat. Working quickly, ladle a scant ¼ cup/60ml of batter into the skillet, then swirl and shake the skillet to evenly coat the bottom with the batter. Return to the heat and cook the crêpe until the underside is light golden brown in spots, about 2 minutes. Slide a spatula underneath to loosen the crêpe and carefully flip it over. Cook on the second side until the batter is just set, about 30 seconds. Transfer to a large plate. Repeat with the remaining batter, wiping the pan with new oil each time. Stack the crêpes on the plate as you go (you should have about six).

4. Once all of the crêpes have been cooked, fold each one into quarters and set aside. In a large skillet over medium heat, whisk together the orange marmalade and orange juice. Cook, stirring occasionally, until the marmalade has melted and the mixture resembles a thick syrup, 6 to 8 minutes. Remove the skillet from the stove and add the orange liqueur. Ignite the alcohol with a long match or a stick lighter. Gently swirl the pan until the flames subside, about 15 seconds.

5. Return the skillet to the stovetop and turn the heat back on to medium. Add the cubes of cold butter, one or two at a time, whisking well after each addition. After the last of the butter has been added, simmer the sauce until it is thick and glossy, about 1 additional minute. If you prefer a slightly thinner sauce, whisk in a splash of water or additional orange juice. Add half of the folded crêpes to the sauce in a single layer and cook until the crêpes are heated through, spooning the hot sauce over the top of the crêpes, about 1 minute. Transfer the crêpes to a serving plate, then repeat with the remaining folded crêpes and place onto a second serving plate.

6. Spoon any remaining sauce over the hot crêpes and top with dollops of sour cream and a light dusting of confectioners' sugar. Serve immediately.

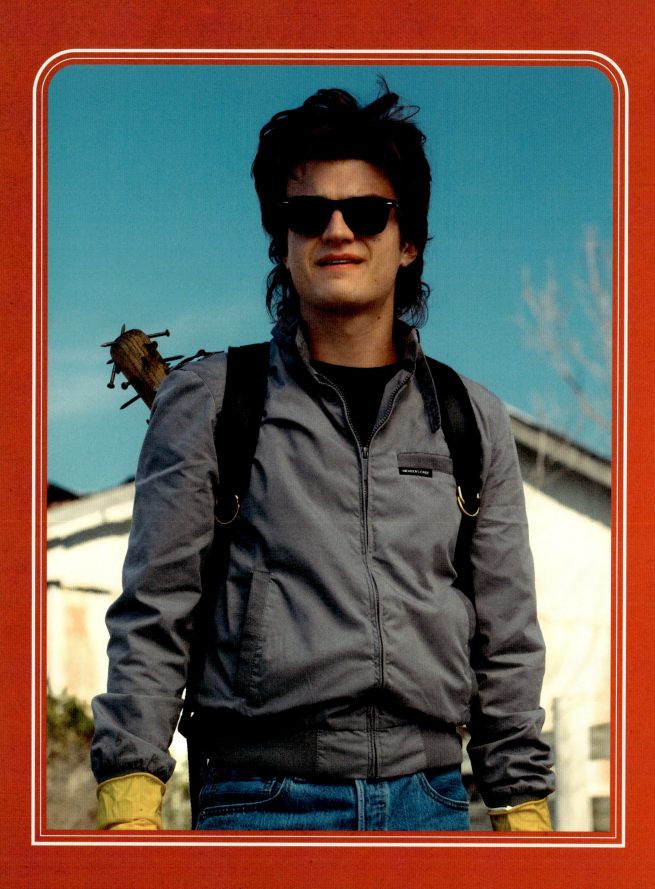

Dart Shots

SERVES 12

What's shimmering green and cute and will eat the face off your cat? It's a Dart shot, inspired by Dustin's adorable Demodog. Just like the Jell-O shots of misbegotten youth—but actually delicious (and good-looking)—these are made to slurp down in the name of interspecies and cross-universe friendship.

Cooking spray

1½ cups / 360ml boiling water, divided

1 (3-ounce / 85g) package green lime-flavored gelatin

1 cup / 240ml vodka or blanco tequila, chilled, divided

1 (3-ounce / 85g) package pink watermelon-flavored gelatin

1½ teaspoons poppy seeds

Special Equipment
12 (3-ounce / 88ml) disposable paper cups

1. Arrange the disposable paper cups on a small baking sheet. Spray a light coating of cooking spray onto a paper towel and wipe the inside of each cup with the oil. Set aside.

2. Divide the boiling water into two medium heatproof bowls (¾ cup / 175ml in each), then whisk the lime-flavored gelatin into one and the watermelon-flavored gelatin into the other, stirring until completely dissolved. Let cool for 10 to 15 minutes, then stir in ½ cup / 120ml of cold vodka or tequila into each bowl.

3. Chill both bowls of gelatin in the refrigerator until they begin to thicken and are the consistency of thick fruit jelly, about 30 minutes, stirring well every 10 minutes.

4. Working quickly, stir the poppy seeds into the lime gelatin (the gelatin should be thick enough that the seeds are suspended in the gelatin). Spoon the lime gelatin evenly into the prepared paper cups (about 1½ tablespoons each). Top with the watermelon gelatin (about 1½ tablespoons each). Use a spoon to gently press down on the top layer of gelatin to ensure that the two layers of gelatin adhere. Chill in the refrigerator until completely set, about 1 hour.

5. Use kitchen shears to cut a small slit in the side of each cup, then gently tear away the paper. Place the shots green-side up onto a serving platter and serve immediately.

COOK'S NOTE

You can create fun shapes by making the gelatin shots in your favorite silicone ice cube molds (a dinosaur- or frog-shaped mold would work particularly well here). Just make sure to rub the cooking spray into the small crevices of your molds to ensure the gelatin shots come out with ease.

If you want to make the shots nonalcoholic, replace the vodka or tequila with apple juice, white grape juice, or white cranberry juice.

Snow Ball Punch

SERVES 8 TO 12 (ABOUT 1 GALLON / 3.8L)

Love is in the air, tinsel is in the auditorium, and The Police are on the crappy speakers. But the real question at 1984's Hawkins Middle School Snow Ball is, What's in the punch bowl? The answer: a refreshing blue beverage—the color of the Hawkins Cubs—with delicious creamy lemonade snowflake ice cubes. So as soon as Mike and Eleven, Dustin and Nancy, and Lucas and Max tire from dancing, they can quench their thirst and get back out there.

Creamy Lemonade Ice Cubes and Frozen Blueberries

¾ cup / 175ml sweetened condensed milk

½ cup / 120ml fresh lemon juice (from about 2 large lemons)

1½ cups / 360ml water

2 cups / 300g large blueberries

Ginger Syrup

One 4-inch / 10cm piece of ginger, peeled and thinly sliced (about ½ cup / 55g)

½ cup / 120ml water

½ cup / 100g granulated sugar

Blue Punch

6 cups / 1.4L white cranberry juice (you can also substitute white grape juice, but the punch will be sweeter), chilled

6 cups / 1.4L lemon-lime soda, chilled

2 cups / 475ml plain seltzer water, chilled

Blue food coloring, as needed

Special Equipment

Two (6-cavity) large snowflake-shaped silicone molds (ideally each cavity should be 3 to 3½ inches / 7.5 to 9cm wide and hold about ½ cup / 120ml of liquid)

1. Make the creamy lemonade ice cubes and frozen blueberries: In a medium bowl, whisk together the sweetened condensed milk, lemon juice, and water until well combined and smooth. Divide the creamy lemonade into 8 cavities of two (6-cavity) large snowflake-shaped silicone molds and freeze until completely firm and frozen. Scatter the blueberries onto a small rimmed baking sheet and freeze alongside the creamy lemonade.

2. Make the ginger syrup: In a small saucepan, combine the ginger, water, and sugar. Stir to combine, then slowly bring to a bare simmer over low heat, stirring occasionally, about 10 minutes. Once the mixture starts to simmer, remove the saucepan from the heat and cool the syrup completely at room temperature.

3. Once cooled, strain the syrup into a small bowl and press down on the ginger to extract as much flavor as possible.

4. Make the blue punch: In an extra-large serving bowl or a punch bowl, combine the ginger syrup, white cranberry juice, lemon-lime soda, and club soda. Stir in drops of blue food coloring until the punch turns a deep shade of blue (10 to 16 drops, depending on your food coloring). Just before serving, add the creamy lemonade ice cubes and frozen blueberries. As the jumbo ice cubes melt, they will turn the punch a milky shade of blue.

COOK'S NOTE

If you can't find snowflake molds, look for molds for extra-large cubes, spheres, or another winter-centric shape—but whatever you choose, look for ones that will hold at least a ½ cup of liquid, as smaller ice cubes will melt too quickly.

CHAPTER THREE

85

SCHOOL'S OUT IN HAWKINS and everyone is down at the mall—that's Starcourt Mall, the massive new addition to the town's landscape. The mall is a teenage dream, where Eleven, Max, Lucas, Mike, and the rest of the gang can be found hanging out, goofing off, and going shopping. It's where Steve has gotten a job slinging ice cream at Scoops Ahoy, and where he meets Robin, his fellow scooper, who is sharp-tongued and quick with the samples. Starcourt is where everyone from Erica Sinclair to Billy Hargrove can be at home. The mall is the new beating heart of Hawkins' social scene, and its food court is its neon-lit nerve center. Where else can you get a hot dog on a stick, Imperial Panda, Teppanyaki, and a USS Butterscotch Sundae all served to you by bored teens in ridiculous uniforms?

But the mall's gain is Main Street's demise. As shopping has been consolidated at Starcourt, shops like Melvald's and restaurants like Enzo's struggle to adapt. Thankfully, Enzo's, with its Chianti in straw baskets, white tablecloths, and candlesticks, offers a level of fine dining well beyond the food court. Enzo's is still where the young—and not so young—lovers of Hawkins gather for romance and Parmesan. And there are other cultural touchstones, like the County Fair, with its colorful booths and culinary competitions, to sate the civic appetite.

Full stomachs will come in handy as Hawkins battles, yet again, the evil forces of not only the Upside Down but the Russians who have surreptitiously established a subterranean laboratory underneath Starcourt Mall. It's that sense of common purpose that Hawkins will need as its youth once again must save not just the town but the world itself. Even as the bonds of their friendships are tested by adolescent drama—girls! boys! long-distance (maybe imaginary) girlfriends!—the Party hangs together. As Starcourt becomes the epicenter of an epic battle between good and evil, as the food court becomes an inferno of burnt hot dogs and incinerated ice cream, as the Mind Flayer claims another victim, the Party steps up to save the world again.

RECIPES

Choco-Banana Muscle Builder Protein Shake

MAKES 1 LARGE OR 2 SMALL SERVINGS (ABOUT 3 CUPS / 720ML TOTAL)

A physique like Billy Hargrove's—a physique that drives Karen Wheeler and the other Hawkins housewives at the pool crazy—doesn't happen without hard work. Sure, he has his bench presses, squats, and bicep curls to thank, but nutrition is key too. Enter Billy's protein shake, which is chock-full of everything he needs to build those muscles. And Adonis or not, who doesn't like a silky chocolate and banana milkshake?

⅓ cup / 75g whole-milk cottage cheese

¾ cup / 175ml milk or milk substitute

1 egg white (optional)

1 medium-ripe banana, sliced into ¼-inch / 6mm rounds and frozen (about 1 cup / 130g)

1 large scoop chocolate protein powder (about ¼ cup / 30g)

1 tablespoon honey

1 cup / 130g ice cubes

1. Combine the cottage cheese, milk, egg white (if using), frozen banana slices, protein powder, honey, and ice cubes in a blender and blend until smooth.

2. Drink it straight from the blender like Billy does.

COOK'S NOTE To make your shake extra chocolaty, add 2 teaspoons unsweetened cocoa powder to the mix before blending.

Nine Flayer Dip

SERVES 8 TO 12

*You can't have a party of the Flayed without a
Nine Flayer Dip, a dish so delicious it will possess
you (with the urge to scoop more of it up). Like
the nefarious Mind Flayer summoning Hawkins'
Flayed back to his side, this dip brings together
disparate entities—cheese, meat, caramelized
onions, fruit, nuts—into one terrifyingly addictive
monster of an appetizer.*

3 tablespoons unsalted butter

2 tablespoons canola oil

4 Spanish onions, halved and thinly sliced

Kosher salt and freshly ground black pepper

¼ cup / 60ml brandy

1½ pounds / 680g whole-milk ricotta cheese

¼ cup / 25g grated Parmesan cheese

¼ cup / 60ml extra-virgin olive oil

2 tablespoons chopped fresh flat-leaf parsley
leaves

4 ounces / 115g goat cheese, at room temperature

12 ounces / 340g cream cheese, at room
temperature

½ cup / 150g hot pepper jelly

6 ounces / 170g salami, cut into ½-inch /
1.3cm pieces

6 ounces / 170g hot sopressata, cut into ½-inch /
1.3cm pieces

8 ounces / 225g sharp white cheddar cheese or
Gruyère cheese, shredded

8 ounces / 225g roasted and salted mixed nuts,
coarsely chopped

8 ounces / 225g Brie cheese, cut into ½-inch /
1.3cm cubes

8 ounces / 225g seedless red and green grapes,
halved or quartered

2 to 3 tablespoons honey

Crackers, crostini, crispy breadsticks (grissini),
and/or sliced apples, for serving

1. In a large Dutch oven, combine the butter and canola oil over medium heat until the butter is melted and starting to foam. Add the onions, season with salt and pepper, and cook, stirring occasionally, until the onions are tender, browned, and starting to stick to the bottom of the pot, 40 to 50 minutes. Add the brandy and, using a wooden spoon, scrape up any browned bits at the bottom of the pot. Continue to cook, stirring occasionally, until the onions are deep golden brown and caramelized, 30 to 50 minutes more. Transfer to a bowl and cool at room temperature.

2. In a medium bowl, combine the ricotta, Parmesan, and olive oil. Season liberally with salt and pepper and whisk until smooth and well combined. Stir in the parsley and set aside.

3. In a large bowl, combine the goat cheese and cream cheese. Using a handheld mixer, blend until smooth and creamy. Spoon into the bottom of a 3-quart / 2.8L clear glass trifle bowl and smooth into an even layer. Using the back of a spoon, create five or six deep divots in the cheese mixture. Fill the divots with the hot pepper jelly and then use a butter knife to swirl the jelly into the cheese. Layer with the salami, sopressata, cheddar, cooled caramelized onions, ricotta mixture, mixed nuts, and Brie. Mound the grapes in the center of the Brie (leaving a roughly 1-inch / 2.5cm border) and then drizzle with the honey.

4. Serve the dip with crackers, crostini, crispy breadsticks, and/or sliced apples.

Suzie,
I miss you and Camp Know Where
already. I'm setting up Cerebro as soon
as I can get to the top of a hill and will
call you on it. But in the meantime, I'm
making those Green Chile Cheeseburgers
I remember from camp. Those were
my favorite and remind me of our
dinners together, dodging mosquitoes and
discussing physics. It is spicy, but your
Dusty-Bun can handle the heat.
I wish I could come to Salt Lake City
to visit and eat cheeseburgers with you, but
for now, this postcard will have to do.
            Over and out.
                    Dusty

Post Card

PLACE
STAMP
HERE

CAMP
'85
KNOW WHERE

MEMORIES

Camp Know Where's Green Chile Cheeseburger

SERVES 4

Dustin will never forget the summer of 1985. It was at Camp Know Where, the sleepaway camp for the scientifically inclined, where Dustin developed a ham radio dubbed Cerebro, an automatic hammer (the Slammer), and feelings for a camper named Suzie Bingham. When they weren't in activities, the Dusty-Bun and Suzie-Poo could be found sharing meals together, notably this Green Chile Cheeseburger, a camper favorite.

12 ounces / 340g Hatch green chiles (4 to 6 total; see Cook's Note)

1 white onion

2 teaspoons canola oil, plus more for the grill

Kosher salt and freshly ground black pepper

4 sesame seed hamburger buns, split

1½ pounds / 680g ground beef (85% lean and 15% fat)

4 slices smoked or sharp cheddar cheese

For serving

Green leaf lettuce, tomato slices, mayonnaise, and yellow mustard

1. Preheat a charcoal grill, gas grill, or cast-iron grill pan to medium-high heat. Arrange the chiles on the grill in a single layer and cook until tender and deeply charred and blackened in spots, 10 to 15 minutes, turning the chiles as needed to ensure even charring. The timing for this will depend heavily on the heat of the grill you are using.

2. Transfer the chiles to a medium bowl, cover the top with plastic wrap, and let steam for 20 minutes. Meanwhile, peel the onion and cut crosswise into four rounds that are a touch thinner than ½ inch / 1.3cm (save any extra onion for another use). Brush the onion rounds with the canola oil and season

with salt and pepper. Grill on both sides until deeply charred in spots and tender, 3 to 5 minutes per side. Transfer to a large baking sheet. Separate the onions into individual rings and set aside. Next, grill the buns cut-side down until lightly toasted and charred in spots, about 30 seconds. Transfer to the same baking sheet as the onions and set aside.

3. After the chiles are finished steaming, remove the skin and seeds, then coarsely chop. Transfer to a small bowl, season with salt, and set aside. Divide the ground beef into four equal portions and form each into a ¾-inch / 2cm-thick patty. Make a ½-inch / 1.3cm-deep and 1-inch / 2.5cm-wide depression in the center of each patty with your thumb. Season both sides of the patties liberally with salt and pepper.

4. Grill the burgers depression-side up until slightly charred and crusty on the first side, about 3 minutes. Flip the burgers and cook until charred on the second side, about 2 minutes more.

5. Lay a slice of cheddar on top of each burger and top evenly with the grilled onions and green chiles. Close the lid to the grill and cook until the cheese is completely melted, 1 to 2 minutes. This timing will yield burgers that are medium-rare, but you can cook the burgers for longer if you prefer your meat medium or well-done.

6. Place the burgers in between the toasted hamburger buns and serve with lettuce, tomato slices, mayonnaise, and mustard on the side so everyone can dress their burger as they like.

COOK'S NOTE

Fresh Hatch green chiles are available only in fall, in and around New Mexico; if you can't get those, you can substitute with ¾ cup / 6 ounces / 170g canned or frozen (and thawed) roasted and chopped Hatch green chiles instead. If you prefer using fresh chiles, Anaheim chiles are a great stand-in but are milder in flavor.

MEMORIES

Alexei's Slurpee

SERVES 4 (ABOUT 7 CUPS / 1.7L TOTAL)

In 1985, the Cold War is raging and it isn't clear who will win. But in the great Slurpee Wars, America is victorious. Even as true a patriot as Alexei, a Russian scientist deeply indoctrinated into Marxist dogma, can't resist the utter frozen joy of a cherry Slurpee from 7-Eleven. (Strawberry is another matter.) This twist on a Slurpee is sweet but uses real cherries (and real strawberries) as well as lemon juice to make a well-balanced and refreshing drink.

1 cup / 34g freeze-dried tart cherries
1 cup / 16g freeze-dried strawberries
½ cup / 100g granulated sugar
1½ cups / 350ml club soda, divided
½ cup / 120ml grenadine syrup
2 tablespoons fresh lemon juice
8 cups / 1kg ice cubes

1. In a large blender, combine the freeze-dried tart cherries, freeze-dried strawberries, and sugar and blend until it is a fine powder consistency (some small bits are fine). Add ¾ cup / 175ml of the club soda, the grenadine syrup, and lemon juice and blend until completely smooth. Add 6 cups / 780g of the ice cubes and the remaining ¾ cup / 175ml club soda and blend until the mixture is just blended but still chunky. Add the remaining 2 cups / 260g ice cubes and blend until smooth and slightly airy in consistency.

2. Pour into four cups and serve immediately.

COOK'S NOTE

For a cherry-cola twist, add a float of chilled cola to the top of the Slurpees, or for a fun play on a Shirley Temple, try a float of chilled lemon-lime soda.

"TELL THAT STUPID MAN IT IS NOT THE SAME IN THE SLIGHTEST, AND I WOULD LIKE THE CHERRY I REQUESTED."

ALEXEI

Hoosier Pork Tenderloin Sandwich

SERVES 4

Every fair has the same food, mostly. Corn dogs (see page 125). Funnel cakes. Popcorn. But only in Indiana will you find pork tenderloin sandwich, a Hoosier specialty. The sandwich comes from the German immigrants who settled the area in the nineteenth century. At home, they made veal schnitzel, but here, where pork is more plentiful than beef, they changed the meat but kept the crunch.

3 eggs
2 cups / 475ml buttermilk
2 teaspoons onion powder, divided
2 teaspoons garlic powder, divided
2 teaspoons chili powder, divided
Kosher salt and freshly ground black pepper
4 (8-ounce / 225g) boneless center-cut pork loin chops (¾ inch / 2cm to 1 inch / 2.5cm thick)
5 ounces / 140g butter crackers, such as Ritz, coarsely crumbled
1½ cups / 180g instant flour, such as Wondra
Canola oil or peanut oil, for frying
4 hamburger buns, split
1½ cups / 110g shredded iceberg lettuce
8 thin beefsteak tomato slices
8 thin red onion slices

For serving
Mayonnaise
Yellow mustard
Sliced dill pickles

1. In a large bowl, whisk together the eggs, buttermilk, 1 teaspoon of the onion powder, 1 teaspoon of the garlic powder, 1 teaspoon of the chili powder, 1¼ teaspoons salt, and ½ teaspoon black pepper. Set aside.

2. Trim any excess fat from around the pork chops, then butterfly them: Lay each chop flat and, using a sharp knife, make a deep cut horizontally from one end to the other, but do not cut all the way through the meat. Open each pork chop like a book, then cover with plastic wrap. Use the flat side of a meat mallet or a rolling pin to pound the meat until it is ¼ inch / 6mm thick and about 7 inches / 18cm wide. Set the pounded chops in the buttermilk marinade, making sure they are well coated on all sides. Cover the bowl with plastic wrap and refrigerate for at least 2 hours and up to overnight.

3. When you are ready to bread the pork, stir together the crumbled butter crackers, instant flour, 1¼ teaspoon salt, ½ teaspoon black pepper, and the remaining 1 teaspoon onion powder, 1 teaspoon garlic powder, and 1 teaspoon chili powder. Place a wire rack on top of a baking sheet and set aside.

4. Remove the marinated pork from the refrigerator. Working with one piece of pork at a time, remove from the buttermilk, shake off any excess, and dredge on both sides in the cracker and flour mixture. Transfer to the wire rack and repeat with the remaining pork. Chill the breaded pork, still on the rack, in the refrigerator for 30 minutes. This will help the breading stick to the pork better during the frying process.

5. When you are ready to fry the pork, fill a large, deep cast-iron skillet halfway with oil and heat to 350°F / 175°C. Place a second wire rack on top of a second baking sheet and set aside (or, if you do not have a second wire rack, line the baking sheet with paper towels). One at a time, fry the dredged pork in the hot oil until golden brown, crispy, and cooked through, about 3 minutes per side. Transfer the fried pork to the second wire rack and season with salt.

6. Layer the bottom of the hamburger buns with the shredded lettuce, tomato, and red onion slices, then top with the fried pork. Cover with the hamburger bun tops and serve immediately with mayonnaise, mustard, and sliced dill pickles on the side.

Roane County Fair Blue Ribbon Sugar Cream Pie

SERVES 8 TO 10

Some call Sugar Cream Pie "Desperation Pie" because you can make it with barely anything. In fact, the only thing sad about this unofficial state pie of Indiana—brought to the state by Quakers who immigrated here in the early 1800s—is when you run out of it. At the Roane County Fair, this pie always get the blue ribbon.

Crust
¼ cup / 55g unsalted butter, cut into cubes
¼ cup / 50g vegetable shortening
1½ cups / 210g all-purpose flour, plus more for dusting
1 tablespoon granulated sugar
¼ teaspoon freshly grated nutmeg
¾ teaspoon kosher salt
¼ cup / 60ml ice water

Filling
¾ cup / 150g granulated sugar
¼ cup / 35g cornstarch
½ teaspoon kosher salt
2½ cups / 590ml heavy cream
6 tablespoons / 85g unsalted butter, cut into cubes
1½ teaspoons vanilla extract
Freshly grated nutmeg, for dusting

1. Make the crust: Put the butter and vegetable shortening into the freezer for 20 minutes.

2. In a large bowl, combine the flour, sugar, nutmeg, and salt. Add the cold butter and vegetable shortening and use a pastry cutter or your fingertips to cut the butter and shortening into the flour until the texture resembles coarse meal. Drizzle 3 tablespoons of the ice water over the flour mixture and use your hands to mix until the dough just starts to come together, adding more water, 1 teaspoon at a time, if needed.

3. Transfer the dough to a large piece of plastic wrap, pressing it mostly smooth, and flatten into a 1-inch / 2.5cm-thick disk. Wrap tightly and let chill in the refrigerator for 1 hour.

4. On a lightly floured work surface, roll the dough into a 12-inch / 30cm round that is a little thinner than ⅛ inch / 3mm.

5. Gently press the dough into a 9-inch / 23cm pie plate and trim the edges, leaving 1 inch / 2.5cm of overhang. Fold the overhanging dough under itself and crimp the edges with your fingers. Pierce the bottom all over with a fork. Refrigerate the crust until it is firm, about 30 minutes.

6. Put a baking sheet onto the center rack of the oven and preheat to 375°F / 190°C. Line the chilled crust with parchment paper or aluminum foil and fill with dry rice or beans or baking weights.

COOK'S NOTE

Because of the heavy cream and butter in this recipe, the pie will set up very firm and be less custardy if it is refrigerated for an extended amount of time. If making it a day ahead, refrigerate it overnight, but make sure to let it sit on the counter for several hours to take the chill off before serving.

For a less-rich pie, use whole milk or half-and-half in place of the heavy cream.

7. Set the pie plate on the hot baking sheet and bake until the edges of the crust start to feel dry and set, 15 to 20 minutes. Carefully remove the parchment paper or foil and the rice, beans, or weights. Return the pie plate to the oven and continue to bake until the edges of the crust are lightly browned in spots and the bottom is dry and cooked through, about 15 minutes more. Remove from the oven and let cool slightly while you make the filling (leave the oven on and the baking sheet in the oven).

8. Make the filling: In a large saucepan, combine the sugar, cornstarch, and salt over medium heat and whisk until smooth. Add the heavy cream, whisk to combine, and then cook, whisking frequently, until the mixture starts to bubble, 7 to 10 minutes. Continue to cook, whisking constantly, until the mixture is thickened to the consistency of pudding, about 1 minute more.

9. Remove from the heat, add the butter and vanilla, and whisk until the butter is completely melted. Transfer to the warm crust and smooth the top with a rubber spatula. Grate a light dusting of fresh nutmeg on top of the custard. Bake on the hot baking sheet until the filling is bubbling and lightly browned in spots, about 20 minutes. It will still be jiggly at this point but will set up as it cools. Remove from the oven and let cool completely (the custard will feel firm to the touch once it is thoroughly cooled) on the baking sheet, 3 to 4 hours.

10. When ready to serve, slice into individual portions.

A Corn Dog for Alexei

MAKES 8 CORN DOGS

If only Alexei had been able to survive Grigori's deadly attack a few more minutes, he would have tasted a corn dog, the greatest of all fair food. But he didn't. Rather, Murray found him, slumped over on the grass. Bereft, he cried for his fallen friend . . . after eating both corn dogs.

1 cup / 150g fresh sweet yellow corn kernels
½ cup / 120ml milk
1 egg
1 tablespoon granulated sugar
Kosher salt
1¼ cups / 175g all-purpose flour, divided
¾ cup / 114g medium-grind yellow cornmeal
1½ teaspoons baking powder
Canola oil, for frying
8 hot dogs
Ketchup, for serving
Yellow mustard, for serving

Special Equipment

8 (8-inch / 20cm) wooden skewers, pointed ends
   cut away

1. In a blender, combine the corn, milk, egg, sugar, and 1 teaspoon salt and blend until completely smooth. Remove the carafe from the blender base and add 1 cup / 140g of the flour, the cornmeal, and baking powder. Using a wooden spoon or rubber spatula, lightly stir the dry ingredients into the corn mixture several times. Return the blender carafe to the base and blend until the mixture is just combined (do not overblend; the batter will be thick). Set the batter aside.

2. Fill a large Dutch oven or pot halfway with canola oil, set over medium-high heat, and bring to 350°F / 175°C. Set a wire rack into a baking sheet. Put the remaining ¼ cup / 35g flour on a plate.

3. Pat the hot dogs very dry with paper towels. Thread one hot dog lengthwise onto a wooden skewer, pushing the skewer almost to the end of the hot dog. Repeat with the remaining hot dogs and skewers. When the oil has reached the desired temperature, hold a prepped hot dog by the skewer, dredge in the flour (tapping off any excess), and dip into the batter (which is still in the blender). Coat the hot dog completely, tipping the blender carafe as needed to make it easier to cover the hot dog with a thick layer of batter.

4. Once coated, gently lay the battered hot dog into the hot oil and fry, turning occasionally, until the batter is deep golden brown and cooked through, 4 to 5 minutes. Working quickly, dredge and batter another two hot dogs, to fry three corn dogs total at a time. As they finish cooking, transfer the fried corn dogs to the prepared rack and season with salt. Dredge, batter, and fry the remaining five corn dogs in two batches.

5. Serve the corn dogs while they are hot, with ketchup and mustard.

COOK'S NOTE Don't waste the leftover batter—you can fry it up to make delicious hush puppies. Drop spoonfuls of the batter into the hot oil and fry until puffed, golden brown, and cooked through, about 3 minutes.

Rocky Robin Brownie Ice Cream Sandwich

SERVES 12 TO 16

Robin Buckley must be the most overqualified ice cream scooper in Scoops Ahoy history. Fluent in four languages (including pig latin), proficient at the French horn, and, as she proves, an adept code breaker, it is no wonder that Buckley can also construct one of the best brownie ice cream sandwiches this side of the Iron Curtain.

Brownie Ice Cream Sandwiches

1 half-gallon / 1.89L container Rocky Road or chocolate ice cream, slightly softened

Cooking spray

1 cup / 140g all-purpose flour

¼ cup / 20g cocoa powder

1 teaspoon kosher salt

1 cup / 220g unsalted butter

8 ounces / 225g semisweet chocolate chips (about 1⅓ cups)

1 cup / 200g granulated sugar

⅓ cup / 65g packed light brown sugar

4 large eggs, at room temperature

2 teaspoons vanilla extract

½ cup / 52g marshmallow crème

1 teaspoon warm water

Hard-Shell Chocolate Sauce and Toppings

8 ounces / 225g semisweet chocolate chips (about 1⅓ cups)

⅓ cup / 75g refined coconut oil

½ cup / 55g toasted sliced almonds

½ cup / 60g toasted chopped walnuts

1. Line a 9 by 13-inch / 23 by 33cm rimmed baking sheet (commonly referred to as a quarter-sheet pan) with two larger overlapping pieces of plastic wrap that have at least 6 inches / 15cm of overhang on each side of the pan. Alternatively, a 9 by 13-inch / 23 by 33cm cake pan or baking dish will also work and will yield similar results. Scoop the ice cream into the lined baking sheet and smooth it down, making sure to reach the corners. Cover it completely with the plastic wrap and use your hands to gently press down evenly on the top so that it is flat. Place in the freezer until completely frozen and firm, at least 4 hours and up to overnight.

2. When ready to bake, set a rack in the center of the oven and preheat to 325°F / 165°C.

3. Line the bottom of an 18 by 13-inch / 45 to 33cm rimmed baking sheet (commonly referred to as a half-sheet pan) with a piece of heavy-duty aluminum foil that is long enough to come up each of the two shorter sides of the baking sheet by 2 inches / 5cm (this will help you lift the brownies out of the pan later). Spray the foil and the two exposed longer sides of the baking sheet with cooking spray and set aside.

4. In a small bowl, whisk together the flour, cocoa powder, and salt, being extra careful to work out any clumps in the cocoa powder. Set aside.

5. In a medium saucepan over low heat, melt the butter until it is hot and steamy (but with no signs of bubbling), about 5 minutes. Remove the saucepan from the heat, add the chocolate chips, then stir with a rubber spatula until the residual heat melts the chocolate. Set the mixture aside to cool slightly for 10 minutes.

RECIPE CONTINUES >>>

"YOU THINK YOU'RE SO SMART, BUT A COUPLE OF KIDS WHO
SCOOP ICE CREAM FOR A LIVING CRACKED YOUR CODE IN A DAY."

ROBIN

6. After 10 minutes, add the granulated sugar and light brown sugar to the chocolate mixture and whisk to combine (it will look grainy). Whisk in the eggs, one at a time, whisking well after each addition, then whisk in the vanilla. Add the flour mixture and stir until just combined.

7. Scrape the batter into the prepared baking sheet and spread it out evenly, making sure to reach the corners of the baking sheet.

8. In a small bowl, stir the marshmallow crème with the warm water until well combined and smooth. It will seem separated at first, but keep on stirring and it will come together. It should be thin enough to drizzle off a spoon in thick ribbons. If not, stir in the tiniest splash of additional warm water to thin it out further. Drizzle the thinned-out crème onto the brownie batter (avoid the edges, as it will cause the brownie to stick to the baking sheet and/or foil), then use a butter knife to swirl it into a marbled pattern in the batter, being careful to not touch the bottom of the batter with the knife.

9. Bake the brownies, rotating the pan 180 degrees after 15 minutes, until the top and edges are set and a cake tester or wooden skewer inserted into the center comes out clean, about 25 minutes total.

10. Remove from the oven, set on a wire rack, and allow to cool in the baking sheet until barely warm, about 30 minutes. Transfer to the refrigerator and chill until cold and firm, at least 1 hour (you can keep it chilled for longer, as the ice cream block still needs time to freeze).

11. When you are ready to assemble, remove the ice cream from the freezer, remove it from the baking sheet, and put the wrapped ice cream block back in the freezer. Line the empty quarter-sheet pan with two larger overlapping pieces of plastic wrap that have at least 8 inches / 20cm of overhang on each side of the pan and set aside. Remove the chilled brownie from the refrigerator and carefully run a paring knife along the long edges of the baking sheet to loosen the brownie from the pan. Pick up the overhanging foil and

gently slide the brownie onto a large cutting board. Use a serrated knife to cut the brownie in half crosswise, being careful not to cut through the foil. Gently lift one side of the foil so that it helps to stand one half of the brownie up on its side. Use one hand to hold the brownie and the other hand to gently peel back the foil, then lift the brownie half and place top-side down into the lined quarter baking sheet (it should fit perfectly inside the rimmed edges).

12. Unwrap the ice cream block and set it on top of the brownie half inside the baking sheet, then top with the second brownie half (top-side up). Wrap the ice cream sandwich in the plastic wrap and use your hands to gently press down on the top to ensure that the ice cream adheres to the brownie halves. Freeze until the brownie halves are completely frozen and firm, at least 2 hours and up to 5 days (the longer the better, to make the sandwiches easier to cut).

13. When the brownie ice cream sandwich is fully frozen, line a half-sheet pan with parchment paper, then cut a smaller piece of parchment paper that will fit inside a quarter-sheet pan and set aside. Remove the large ice cream sandwich from the freezer, unwrap it (but hold onto the plastic wrap), and place it on a cutting board. Use a serrated knife dipped in hot water (and a little bit of brute force) to cut the large sandwich in half crosswise, cleaning the blade of the knife every time you make a cut. Wrap one half in the plastic wrap and return it to the freezer. Line the quarter-sheet pan with the piece of parchment paper you cut previously.

14. Use the serrated knife to cut the remaining half into eight (2 by 3-inch / 5 to 7.5cm) or six (2 by 4-inch / 5 by 10cm) smaller ice cream sandwiches, cleaning the blade of the knife every time you make a cut. Place the sandwiches onto the prepared quarter-sheet pan, then place back in the freezer. Remove the second half, repeat the cutting process, place onto the second prepared baking sheet, and freeze along with the first set of sandwiches while you make the hard-shell chocolate sauce.

15. For the hard-shell chocolate sauce and toppings: In a medium microwave-safe bowl, combine the chocolate chips and coconut oil and warm in the microwave in 20-second intervals, stirring well in between each interval, until mostly melted (a few unmelted chips is fine), about 2 minutes. Remove the bowl from the microwave and stir until completely melted and smooth (the residual heat should help to fully melt the chocolate, but you can put it back in the microwave for several seconds if needed).

16. Transfer the chocolate sauce to a 2-cup / 475ml liquid measuring cup or another cup of similar size and set aside until cooled but still fluid, about 15 minutes. Working with half of the ice cream sandwiches at a time (keep the other half of the ice cream sandwiches in the freezer), dip a sandwich about halfway into the chocolate sauce, allowing any excess to drip back into the cup, and lay the dipped sandwich back on the parchment-lined baking sheet. Sprinkle the top of the sandwich with some almonds and/or walnuts. You can sprinkle half of the sandwiches with almonds and the other half with walnuts or do a combo of both nuts on all the sandwiches. When you've dipped the whole first tray of sandwiches, place them back in the freezer and dip the remaining sandwiches. Allow the dipped sandwiches to sit in the freezer until the chocolate sauce is set, about 5 minutes, then serve.

COOK'S NOTE Pour any leftover hard-shell chocolate sauce (about ½ cup / 120ml) into a small food storage container and store in the refrigerator for up to 2 weeks. To use, heat it in the microwave until it is just melted and use as a fun ice cream topping.

USS Butterscotch Sundae

SERVES 4

Most come for a scoop in a cone or a cup. Some come for two and a few for three. But the true fans of Scoops Ahoy are those who opt for the decadent USS Butterscotch Sundae, the shop's signature treat. The USS Butterscotch is a symphony of sensations, a flotilla of flavor, the highest form ice cream can take.

Strawberry Sauce

8 ounces / 225g strawberries, hulled and thinly sliced

3 tablespoons granulated sugar

Pinch of kosher salt

1½ teaspoons cornstarch

3 tablespoons water

1 tablespoon strawberry preserves

2 teaspoons fresh lemon juice

Butterscotch Sauce

¾ cup / 150g packed dark brown sugar

½ teaspoon kosher salt

⅓ cup / 80ml heavy cream

¼ cup / 55g unsalted butter, cut into small cubes

3 tablespoons dark corn syrup

1 tablespoon Scotch whiskey

1 teaspoon vanilla extract

Hot Fudge Sauce

2 tablespoons unsalted butter, cut into small cubes

⅓ cup / 65g packed dark brown sugar

2 tablespoons unsweetened cocoa powder

Pinch of kosher salt

⅔ cup / 160ml heavy cream

3 tablespoons dark corn syrup

4 ounces / 115g semisweet chocolate, chopped

1½ teaspoons vanilla extract

Whipped Cream

⅔ cup / 160ml heavy cream, chilled

3 tablespoons confectioners' sugar

½ teaspoon vanilla extract

Sundae Assembly

4 bananas, peeled and halved lengthwise

1 pint / 473ml butterscotch, toffee, or dulce de leche ice cream

1 pint / 473ml chocolate ice cream

1 pint / 473ml strawberry ice cream

8 butter waffle cookies or butter crisps

2 tablespoons multicolor sprinkles

12 maraschino cherries

Special Equipment

4 glass or plastic banana split boats

1 large piping bag fitted with a large star tip

1. **Make the strawberry sauce:** In a small saucepan, combine the strawberries, granulated sugar, and salt. Stir to combine and set aside, stirring occasionally, until the sugar and salt dissolve and the strawberries release their juices, about 20 minutes.

2. Once the strawberries are juicy, in a small bowl, mix the cornstarch with the water until dissolved, then add to the saucepan and stir to combine with the strawberries. Turn the heat to medium and cook, stirring frequently, until the mixture comes to a simmer, about 3 minutes. Continue to cook, adjusting the heat as needed to maintain a simmer and stirring frequently, until the strawberries are very tender and the cooking liquid is deep red, thickened, and glossy, 6 to 8 more minutes. Remove from the heat and add the strawberry preserves and lemon juice. Stir until the preserves have completely melted into the sauce. Transfer the strawberry sauce to a bowl and leave at room temperature to cool completely.

RECIPE CONTINUES »»

3. Make the butterscotch sauce: In a medium saucepan, combine the dark brown sugar, salt, heavy cream, butter, and corn syrup. Stir to combine and turn the heat to medium-high. Bring to a boil, stirring frequently, then lower the heat slightly and cook (the mixture should still be vigorously bubbling), still stirring, until the sauce thickens and coats the back of a rubber spatula or wooden spoon, about 5 more minutes. Remove from the heat and stir in the whiskey and vanilla. Transfer the butterscotch sauce to a bowl and cool slightly at room temperature, stirring occasionally. The sauce will thicken further as it cools. It should be served while it is still slightly warm but not hot.

4. Make the hot fudge sauce: In a medium saucepan, combine the butter, brown sugar, cocoa powder, salt, heavy cream, and corn syrup. Bring to a simmer over medium heat, whisking frequently, 3 to 5 minutes. Reduce the heat to low and add the chopped chocolate. Whisk until the chocolate is completely melted and the sauce is smooth and glossy, about 1 minute.

5. Remove from the heat and whisk in the vanilla. Transfer the hot fudge sauce to a bowl and cool slightly at room temperature, stirring occasionally. The sauce will thicken further as it cools. It should be served while it is still slightly warm but not hot.

6. Make the whipped cream: In a large bowl, combine the heavy cream, confectioners' sugar, and vanilla. Use a handheld mixer to blend on low speed until the ingredients are incorporated, then whip on medium-high speed until medium-stiff peaks form. Transfer the whipped cream to a large piping bag fitted with a large star tip.

7. Assemble the sundae: For each sundae, lay two banana halves into a glass or plastic banana split boat. Place a large scoop each of the butterscotch ice cream, chocolate ice cream, and strawberry ice cream in between the banana halves. Nestle one butter waffle cookie between each scoop of ice cream (two cookies per sundae). Drizzle a spoonful of the butterscotch sauce on top of the butterscotch ice cream, chocolate sauce on the chocolate ice cream, and strawberry sauce on the strawberry ice cream. Pipe a small mound of whipped cream on top of the sauce on each scoop of ice cream, then top the whipped cream with some of the sprinkles and a maraschino cherry (three cherries per sundae). Serve immediately.

COOK'S NOTE Store any leftover hot fudge or butterscotch sauce in airtight containers in the refrigerator for up to 2 weeks. To use, warm the sauces ever so slightly in the microwave or on the stovetop until they easily drizzle off a spoon.

Store any leftover strawberry sauce in an airtight container in the refrigerator for up to 5 days. Serve the sauce chilled. If it becomes too thick in the refrigerator, stir in a splash of water to loosen it up.

"AHOY, LADIES. DIDN'T SEE YOU THERE. WOULD YOU LIKE TO SET SAIL ON THIS OCEAN OF FLAVOR WITH ME?"

STEVE

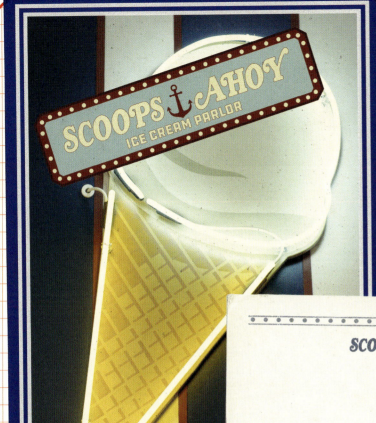

Dingus,

How hard is it to make a sundae?
Answer: <u>not very</u>. Yet I just had to
refund a very upset 11-year-old whose
USS Butterscotch had no butterscotch.
Steve, it's not a butterscotch sundae
if it doesn't have butterscotch in it.

Get it together, dude.   —Robin

Snickerdoodle Cookie Cake

MAKES 1 (APPROXIMATELY 10-INCH / 25CM) COOKIE CAKE

The dead have tombstones. The ancients had tablets. Let the living celebrate milestones with giant cookies, sold at the Starcourt Mall and decorated with messages written in frosting. Birthdays. Graduations. Cries for help. They are all more trenchant when written atop a soft and chewy oversized mall cookie, topped with a delicious cinnamon buttercream frosting.

3 tablespoons granulated sugar, plus ½ cup / 100g, divided

¾ teaspoon ground cinnamon

1½ cups / 210g all-purpose flour

¾ teaspoon cream of tartar

½ teaspoon baking soda

½ teaspoon kosher salt

10 tablespoons / 150g unsalted butter, at room temperature

¼ cup / 50g packed light brown sugar

1 large egg, at room temperature

1 large egg yolk, at room temperature

1½ teaspoons vanilla extract

Cinnamon Buttercream Frosting, for decorating (recipe follows)

Green, yellow, and blue food coloring, as needed

Multicolor sprinkles, for decorating

Special Equipment
2 piping bags

1. Line a large rimmed baking sheet with parchment paper and set aside.

2. In a small bowl, stir together 3 tablespoons of the granulated sugar and the cinnamon, then set aside. In a medium bowl, whisk together the flour, cream of tartar, baking soda, and salt, then set aside.

3. In a large bowl, use an electric hand mixer set on medium-high speed to beat the butter, the remaining ½ cup / 100g granulated sugar, and the brown sugar until light and fluffy, about 3 minutes. Beat in the whole egg, then scrape down the sides of the bowl. Add the egg yolk and vanilla and beat until well combined, light, and almost creamy in texture, about 1 minute. Reduce the mixer speed to low, then add the flour mixture, in two batches, and beat until just combined.

4. Use a rubber spatula to scrape the dough together into a mound in the bowl, then pat it down into a roughly 1-inch / 2.5cm-thick disk and sprinkle it all over with half of the cinnamon sugar, using the spatula to help you flip the mound over to get the cinnamon sugar on all sides. This step will be a bit messy and it won't look neat, but that's okay. Use your hands to transfer the dough onto the prepared baking sheet. Wash your hands and dry them well, then use your clean hands to press the dough into an 8½-inch / 22cm round, about ½ inch / 1.3cm thick. Take your time here and make sure to smooth out the cookie dough and make sure that it is nice and round. The cookie will spread but mostly hold its shape while baking, so how you shape it is important. Chill in the refrigerator until the dough is firm, 30 to 45 minutes.

5. After 30 minutes, set a rack in the center of the oven and preheat to 375° / 190°C.

6. Once the oven is preheated, use your hands to gently flip the dough round over (peeling off the parchment paper as needed and setting the paper back on the baking sheet) and sprinkle with half of the remaining cinnamon sugar, lightly rubbing and pressing the sugar into the dough. Flip the cookie over again so that the top side is facing up again (if some of the cinnamon sugar comes off, spread it out to the same size as the cookie, then set the cookie on top of the sugar) and sprinkle the top with all the remaining cinnamon sugar, lightly rubbing and pressing the sugar into the dough.

RECIPE CONTINUES >>>

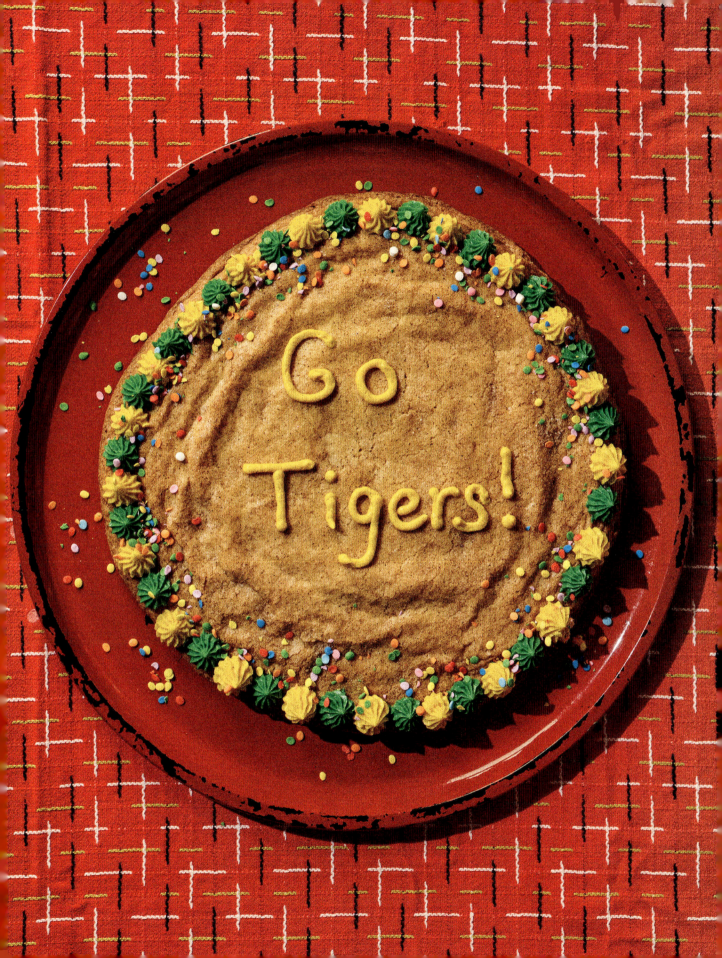

7. Bake until the cookie is light golden brown, the center is set, and the edges are crispy and crackly, 20 to 25 minutes, rotating the baking sheet 180 degrees after 15 minutes. Transfer the baking sheet to a rack and let the cookie cool completely on the pan.

8. While the cookie is cooling, divide the Cinnamon Buttercream Frosting into two small bowls. Stir green food coloring (6 to 12 drops; add several drops of blue for a darker green hue) into one bowl of buttercream and yellow food coloring (6 to 12 drops) into the other bowl of buttercream.

9. Transfer the two frostings into two piping bags fitted with the tips of your choice. Decorate the top of the cooled cookie as you wish (maybe write a fun message or a cry for help, whichever seems more fitting) and scatter on sprinkles if the mood strikes you.

Cinnamon Buttercream Frosting

MAKES ABOUT 3 CUPS / 600G

1 cup / 220g unsalted butter, cut into ½-inch / 1.3cm cubes, at room temperature
3¼ cups / 390g confectioners' sugar, sifted, divided
1½ teaspoons vanilla extract
½ teaspoon ground cinnamon
½ teaspoon kosher salt
3 tablespoons heavy cream, plus more as needed

1. In a large bowl, blend the butter with an electric hand mixer set on medium-low speed until smooth and lightly fluffy, about 2 minutes. Add half of the confectioners' sugar and the vanilla, cinnamon, and salt and blend on low speed until mostly combined.

2. Add the remaining confectioners' sugar and blend on low speed until well combined, then increase the speed to medium-high and blend until smooth and creamy, 2 to 3 minutes. Scrape down the sides of the bowl and blend in the heavy cream on low speed, then increase the speed to medium-high and blend until the frosting is light and fluffy, about 3 more minutes. If the frosting is a touch thick and you think it might be hard to use for piping, loosen up the frosting by adding an additional small splash of heavy cream and blending again until fully incorporated.

Homemade Orange Julius

After you get your ears pierced at Claire's, buy your shoes at Kaufman's, and get sweaty at Jazzercise, what better way to quench your thirst than with the ultimate mall beverage, an Orange Julius? Creamy, tart, and sweet, an Orange Julius—or this homemade version of one—is just the thing for the parched, the exhausted, and the bored.

4 cups / 950ml fresh orange juice, strained of any pulp (see Cook's Note), plus 4 to 6 orange slices (optional)

⅔ cup / 130g granulated sugar

2 cups / 475ml milk

1 tablespoon vanilla extract

5 cups / 750g ice cubes

1. In a medium saucepan, combine the orange juice and sugar. Bring to a boil, then turn the heat to a strong simmer and cook, stirring occasionally, until reduced to 1½ cups (360ml), about 1 hour. Transfer to a bowl and let cool at room temperature for 30 minutes, then refrigerate until completely chilled, about 1 hour. It will thicken up a lot as it cools and set up almost like jam.

2. In a blender, combine the chilled orange juice concentrate, milk, and vanilla and blend until thoroughly combined and smooth. Add the ice and blend again until smooth. Depending on the size of your blender, this might have to be done in two batches.

3. Divide among four tall glasses or six short glasses, garnish each with an orange slice, if desired, and serve immediately.

COOK'S NOTE

Instead of squeezing your own orange juice, you can use store-bought orange juice. Just make sure that it has no added sugar and is pulp-free.

...NITY NEWSPAPER

...okins Post

...A, SUNDAY, OCTOBER 6, 1985

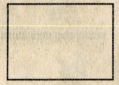

RESTAURANTS

Enzo's on Main Street Still Enchants

By S. MALARKEY

HAWKINS - Hawkins' Main Street is a long way away from Italy, but Enzo's restaurant feels like a true Italian restaurant. Many patrons come simply for the welcoming atmosphere—and strong martinis—but many more come for the offerings from the kitchen. Enzo's Caesar salad is prepared tableside, a dramatic performance worth a screening at the Hawk. The bucatini all'amatriciana, bursting with Calabrian chili, is a meaty and spicy masterpiece. You won't find a better wine list than Enzo's, which boasts not just Piedmontese barolos and Tuscan Chianti but seldom-seen Calabrian selections like Cirò Rosso, made from the gaglioppo grape. However, it's a relatively new addition to the menu, the tiramisu, that has been proved to be a bestseller. Served in a martini glass, the chic presentation has witnessed thousands of first kisses and wedding proposals. The waiters at Enzo's know things are going well when the table also orders the other house specialty: an espresso affogato, a dessert which makes ample use of hazelnut liqueur, gelato (a type of Italian ice cream) and a shot of espresso. "After that, the signora always says, 'I do'!" says an Enzo waiter, grinning. "It's amore!"

MEMORIES

Enzo's
Tiramisu
PAGE 144

I Dolci d'Enzo

There's a reason why Hop wants to meet Joyce at Enzo's. It is quite simply the most romantic restaurant in Hawkins. Though everything from the antipasti to the secondi is delizioso, it's the desserts like tiramisu and an affogato that keep the regulars coming back to Enzo's. If only Joyce had shown up, she would have been swept off her feet in a storm of sweetness.

Enzo's Tiramisu

SERVES 4

1½ tablespoons granulated sugar, plus ¼ cup / 50g, divided

2 tablespoons instant espresso powder

Small pinch of kosher salt

¾ cup / 175ml boiling water

3 tablespoons coffee liqueur, such as Kahlúa

2 egg yolks

2 tablespoons dry or sweet Marsala wine (depending on your sweetness preference)

½ cup / 120ml heavy cream, cold

1 (8-ounce / 225g) container mascarpone cheese, at room temperature

12 to 18 ladyfingers, halved crosswise (see Cook's Note)

Unsweetened cocoa powder, for dusting

Shaved bittersweet chocolate, for topping

Special Equipment
4 large martini glasses

Store-bought ladyfingers come in a range of sizes. Some will be thinner, thicker, shorter, longer, etc. Any size will work as long as you use enough to create distinct layers in between the mascarpone cream.

1. In a medium bowl, whisk together 1½ tablespoons of the sugar, the espresso powder, and salt. Add the boiling water and whisk until the sugar, espresso powder, and salt are completely dissolved. Set the liquid aside. When it has cooled slightly, stir in the coffee liqueur. This will be your espresso soak for the cookies.

2. To make the zabaglione, fill a medium saucepan with 1 inch / 2.5cm of water and bring to a gentle simmer over medium heat. In a medium heatproof bowl, whisk together the egg yolks and remaining ¼ cup / 50g sugar until well combined. Whisk in the Marsala wine until smooth. Set the bowl over the saucepan (make sure that the bowl sits above the level of the simmering water). Whisk constantly until the mixture becomes pale and fluffy and nearly doubles in volume, about 5 minutes, scraping down the sides of the bowl occasionally with the sides of the whisk. The consistency should be similar to thick hollandaise sauce. Remove the bowl from the heat and continue whisking until the mixture is slightly cooled, about 1 minute. Cover loosely with plastic wrap and set aside to cool completely at room temperature. It will continue to thicken as it cools.

3. In a large bowl, whisk the heavy cream until stiff peaks form. Alternatively, use a handheld mixer for this step, but since it is not a large amount of cream, it should whip up pretty quickly by hand. Transfer the whipped cream to a small bowl. To the same large bowl (no need to clean it out), add the mascarpone cheese and use a rubber spatula to stir until the cheese is smooth. Add the cooled zabaglione and whisk until well combined and smooth. Add the whipped cream and use a rubber spatula to fold the cream into the mascarpone and zabaglione until smooth and just combined.

4. Fill the bottom of four large martini glasses with 2 tablespoons of the mascarpone cream and smooth with the back of a spoon. Individually dip two or three ladyfinger halves in the reserved espresso soak until moistened but not soggy, about 2 seconds, and arrange in a single layer on top of the mascarpone cream. Spoon 3 tablespoons of mascarpone cream on top of the ladyfingers and smooth with the back of a spoon. Individually dip four to six additional ladyfinger halves and arrange on top of the mascarpone cream. Top with a final layer of the remaining mascarpone cream (about 3 tablespoons per martini glass) and smooth with the back of a spoon. Loosely cover each glass with plastic wrap and refrigerate for at least 4 hours and up to overnight.

5. When ready to serve, top each tiramisu with a light dusting of cocoa powder and sprinkle with shaved bittersweet chocolate. Serve immediately.

Espresso Affogato

SERVES 4

1½ cups / 360ml vanilla bean gelato
1½ cups / 360ml coffee gelato
4 (1-ounce / 30ml) shots fresh hot espresso
3 tablespoons almond- or hazelnut-flavored liqueur (such as amaretto or Frangelico)
Your favorite biscotti, for serving

1. In four glass mugs, scoop alternating small mounds of vanilla and coffee gelato (two scoops of each flavor in each glass).

2. Pour one shot of hot espresso on top of the gelato in each glass, then top with the liqueur. Serve immediately with your favorite biscotti on the side for dipping.

COOK'S NOTE If you do not have an espresso maker at home, you can also use 1½ ounces / 45ml of very strong coffee or buy espresso from your favorite coffee shop and re-warm at home.

CHAPTER FOUR

WITH THE STARCOURT MALL destroyed in a mysterious fire, our Hawkins heroes begin to scatter. The Byers family—plus Eleven—decamp to Lenora Hills in sunny Southern California, looking for a fresh start. Though unwilling, Jim Hopper is in the frozen tundra of Kamchatka, deep in the USSR (though just across the Bering Strait from Alaska). And at home in Indiana, the bonds of friendship that once held Will, Lucas, and Dustin together have begun to fray.

From Will's den to the Starcourt Food Court to the highly political cafeteria at Hawkins High, the Party seems at an inflection point. Lucas joins the basketball team, on his way to becoming a full-fledged jock; Will and Dustin, on the other hand, join the Hellfire Club, the high school Dungeons & Dragons club presided over by an outrageous longhair named Eddie Munson. Erica, Lucas Sinclair's brilliant younger sister, shows herself to be more than ready to join the Hellfire Club as well. Max, who has lost her friend Eleven to California and her stepbrother, Billy, to the Mind Flayer, is struggling. Robin and Steve have traded their jaunty Scoops Ahoy uniforms for Family Video name tags: less ice cream, more popcorn. Then Vecna appears with a vendetta against the town, wrenching apart several unfortunate residents with sickening power.

Though old friendships might be fraying in Hawkins, new ones are forming elsewhere. Jonathan finally finds a best friend in Argyle, a cheerful stoner who is Surfer Boy Pizza's number one employee. Argyle is the guide to all things SoCal, from the breakfast burritos to the weed. Languishing in a gulag, Hopper deploys his charisma to befriend a prison guard named Dmitri Antonov to help him escape. Joyce reconnects with Murray, and together they make the dubious acquaintance of a hustling peanut butter smuggler named Yuri. And with each new friend—or enemy—comes a new culinary world: Argyle's filling California breakfast burrito, the steaming pirozhki about which Dmitri, imprisoned after the escape is thwarted, dreams, and the Beef Stroganoff of the prisoners' last supper before they are fed to the Demogorgon. Every new adventure is a new flavor.

RECIPES

"THIS IS HELLFIRE CLUB. NOT BABYSITTING CLUB."

EDDIE

DUSTIN, WHAT WAS
THAT CAKE YOU BROUGHT TO
THE LAST MEETING OF THE
HELLFIRE CLUB? IT WAS
INSANE. YOU HAVE TO
BRING IT TO THE NEXT
MEETING. THAT'S AN ORDER.
EITHER WE EAT CAKE OR A
DRAGON EATS YOU.

Hellfire Club Devil's Food Cake

SERVES 8 TO 12

As they battle in the Cult of Vecna campaign, the members of the Hellfire Club also have to eat. Thankfully, between Dustin, Lucas, Mike, Jeff, Gareth, and now Erica, the club is well provisioned with baked goods. Though none has left such an impression on Eddie as Dustin's Hellfire Club Devil's Food Cake, for which we have the always-game Claudia Henderson to thank.

Cake
Cooking spray
1 cup / 220g unsalted butter
1 cup / 240ml stout beer (preferably a chocolate stout)
1 cup / 80g unsweetened Dutch-process cocoa powder
2½ cups / 350g all-purpose flour
1 teaspoon baking powder
1 teaspoon baking soda
1 teaspoon kosher salt
1¾ cups / 400g packed dark brown sugar
1 cup / 240g sour cream, at room temperature
½ cup / 120ml canola oil
1 tablespoon pure vanilla extract
3 eggs, at room temperature
6 ounces / 170g mini semisweet chocolate chips (about a scant 1¼ cups)

Chocolate Glaze
6 ounces / 170g semisweet chocolate chips (about 1 cup)
¼ to ½ teaspoon cayenne pepper, plus more for dusting
¾ cup / 175ml heavy cream

1. Preheat the oven to 350°F / 180°C. Spray a 12-cup / 2.8L nonstick Bundt pan liberally with cooking spray and set the pan on a baking sheet.

2. **Make the cake:** In a medium saucepan, combine the butter and stout over medium heat. Cook, stirring occasionally, until the butter is melted and the mixture comes to a simmer, about 10 minutes. Remove from the heat, add the cocoa powder, and whisk until smooth. Set aside to cool for 30 minutes, whisking occasionally. It is ready to use when it is barely warm and the consistency is similar to thick but pourable chocolate sauce. In a medium bowl, whisk together the flour, baking powder, baking soda, and salt.

3. In a large bowl, whisk together the brown sugar, sour cream, canola oil, and vanilla until smooth. Add the eggs one at a time, whisking well after each addition. In three additions, use a rubber spatula to stir in the flour mixture, alternating with two additions of the slightly cooled beer-and-cocoa mixture, and stirring until the batter is just combined. If the batter is slightly lumpy, whisk it several times until it becomes smooth, but do not overmix. Use a rubber spatula to fold in the mini chocolate chips.

4. Scrape the batter into the prepared pan. Bake, rotating the baking sheet once after 30 minutes, until the top of the cake is puffed and cracked and a cake tester or wooden skewer inserted into the center comes out clean, about 1 hour. Line a baking sheet with parchment paper or a silicone mat and set a wire rack inside of it. Transfer the cake to the wire rack and let cool for 15 minutes, still in the pan. After the cake has cooled slightly, invert the cake out onto the wire rack and cool completely.

RECIPE CONTINUES >>>

5. Make the glaze: In a medium bowl, stir together the chocolate chips and cayenne pepper.

6. In a small saucepan, warm the heavy cream over medium heat, stirring occasionally, until it is very hot and steamy but not yet simmering, 5 to 8 minutes. Pour the hot cream over the chocolate chips and gently shake the bowl so the chocolate is submerged. Let sit for 2 minutes, then stir until completely smooth.

7. Pour the chocolate glaze over the cooled cake, using a rubber spatula or spoon to push the glaze down the sides and center of the cake. Let it sit until the glaze is ever so slightly set (it's ready once the glaze is no longer dripping), 15 to 20 minutes. Transfer the glazed cake to a serving platter or cake stand, dust with additional cayenne pepper, slice into wedges, and serve.

Argyle's Chorizo Breakfast Burrito

SERVES 4

While it's true El might not fit in to the social scene at Lenora Hills High School, the food in sunny Southern California is a major step up from Hawkins. Take, for instance, this spicy chorizo breakfast burrito, first introduced to the Byers family by Argyle, the ultimate arbiter of all things California. It sure beats regular scrambled eggs and comes in a close second after Eggo waffles.

12 ounces / 340g Yukon Gold potatoes, unpeeled, cut into ½-inch / 1.3cm cubes

Kosher salt

¼ cup / 60ml canola oil, divided

8 ounces / 225g coarsely ground fresh Mexican chorizo

1 red onion, coarsely chopped

½ red bell pepper, coarsely chopped

Freshly ground black pepper

6 eggs

3 tablespoons milk

1 tablespoon unsalted butter

1 to 2 tablespoons finely chopped pickled jalapeños

3 tablespoons crumbled cotija cheese

⅔ cup / 70g grated Monterey Jack cheese

4 large burrito-size flour tortillas (at least 10 inches / 25cm)

1 avocado, sliced

3 tablespoons sliced scallions (white and green parts)

Salsa, for serving

Sour cream, for serving

Hot sauce, for serving

1. Line a small baking sheet or large plate with a couple layers of paper towels. Fill a large saucepan halfway full of water, then add the potatoes. Bring to a boil, season the water liberally with salt, lower the heat to medium, and cook until the potatoes are just tender (a fork should go through with some resistance), about 5 minutes. Drain well, then arrange the potatoes in a single layer on the prepared baking sheet. Set aside to cool.

2. Preheat the oven to 300°F / 150°C.

3. In a large cast-iron skillet over medium-high heat, warm 2 tablespoons of the canola oil. Once the oil starts to shimmer, add the chorizo and cook, using a wooden spoon to break up the meat, until browned and cooked through, 6 to 8 minutes. Use a slotted spoon to transfer the cooked chorizo to a small bowl. Add the onion to the skillet and cook, stirring occasionally, until crisp-tender, 3 to 5 minutes. Add the bell pepper and cook, stirring occasionally, until the bell pepper is crisp-tender, 3 to 5 minutes. Increase the heat slightly, add the remaining 2 tablespoons oil and the potatoes, and season with salt and pepper. Stir to combine, then spread the vegetables out so they are in a single layer in the skillet. Cook, flipping and stirring the vegetables occasionally, until the potatoes are browned and crispy in spots, 10 to 12 minutes. Do not flip and stir the vegetables too much, as it will prevent the potatoes from getting browned and crispy. Stir in the cooked chorizo and season with additional salt and pepper if needed. Put the skillet into the oven to keep the chorizo hash warm while you cook the eggs.

4. In a medium bowl, combine the eggs and milk, season with salt and pepper, and whisk vigorously until pale yellow in color and almost foamy.

COOK'S NOTE

Coarsely ground fresh Mexican chorizo works best for this recipe because it cooks up into large crumbles. Some fresh chorizo is very finely ground, which cooks up differently and will change the look and taste of the finished breakfast burritos.

5. In a medium nonstick skillet over medium heat, melt the butter until it starts to lightly bubble and become foamy. Add the eggs and cook, using a heat-resistant rubber spatula to gently stir and scrape as needed, until large, fluffy curds form but the eggs are still a touch wet, 4 to 6 minutes. Remove the eggs from the heat and sprinkle with the jalapeños and half of the cotija and Monterey Jack. Stir gently to combine, then sprinkle with the remaining cotija and Monterey Jack. Cover the skillet to melt the cheese and keep the scrambled eggs warm while you build the burritos.

6. Heat a large skillet over medium heat. Add a tortilla and warm it on both sides until the tortilla is pliable, several seconds per side. Transfer the warm tortilla to a large plate and cover with a clean kitchen towel. Warm the remaining tortillas, stacking the tortillas as they come off the stovetop so that they stay warm.

7. Lay one of the warm tortillas on a cutting board. Shingle a quarter of the sliced avocado toward the bottom of the tortilla and season with salt. Sprinkle the scallions on top of the chorizo hash, then top the sliced avocado with a quarter of the hash and a quarter of the scrambled eggs. Fold in the two sides of the tortilla and roll up tightly from the bottom to the top. Repeat with the remaining tortillas and burrito fillings.

8. Serve the burritos immediately with salsa, sour cream, and hot sauce on the side.

"HOLD ON TO YOUR BUTTS, BROCHACHOS!"

ARGYLE

Surfer Boy Pizza

MAKES 2 (11-INCH / 28CM) PIZZAS

It may have taken some convincing, but the California contingent of the Hawkins kids have become Hawaiian pizza fanatics. With Argyle as the main apostle, they've fallen hard for the mash-up of flavors: cheese, ham, pineapple, peppers. Developed in the '60s by a Greek-born Canadian named Sam Panopoulos, the pie was influenced by Chinese sweet-and-sour flavor combinations with an Italian undercurrent. It's Surfer Boy Pizza's bestselling pizza, and this recipe shows why.

1¼ cups / 300ml warm water

1½ tablespoons honey

1 (¼-ounce/ 7g) packet active dry yeast

½ cup / 120ml extra-virgin olive oil, divided, plus more for brushing

3½ cups / 490g all-purpose flour, plus more for dusting

Kosher salt

1¼ teaspoons granulated garlic

¼ cup / 25g grated Parmesan cheese, plus 2 tablespoons, divided

2 garlic cloves, minced

1 (15-ounce / 425g) can crushed tomatoes

¼ teaspoon granulated sugar

½ teaspoon dried oregano

Pinch of crushed red pepper flakes

1 jalapeño, thinly sliced into rounds

¾ cup / 85g shredded whole milk, low-moisture mozzarella cheese

¾ cup / 90g shredded provolone cheese

4 slices Canadian bacon, cut into bite-size wedges

6 ounces / 115g fresh pineapple, cut into bite-size pieces

1. In a medium bowl, whisk together the warm water and honey. Sprinkle the yeast on top, then set aside until foamy, about 10 minutes. Whisk in 3 tablespoons of the olive oil.

2. In a large bowl, whisk together the flour, 1½ teaspoons salt, and the granulated garlic. Make a well in the center of the flour and pour in the yeast mixture. Gradually stir with a rubber spatula or wooden spoon until a rough dough forms. Sprinkle ¼ cup / 25g of the Parmesan on top of the dough and stir until combined (the dough will still be quite shaggy at this point).

3. On a lightly floured work surface, knead the dough until it is smooth and elastic, about 5 minutes, dusting with more flour if needed. Divide the dough in two, then roll each into a ball. Brush two large bowls with 1 tablespoon of the remaining oil, add a dough ball to each, and turn to coat well with the oil. Cover the bowls tightly with plastic wrap and set aside at room temperature until the dough balls are doubled in size, about 1½ hours.

4. Meanwhile, in a small saucepan over medium heat, add 2 tablespoons of the remaining oil and the minced garlic. Cook, stirring constantly, until the garlic is softened, 1 to 2 minutes. Add the crushed tomatoes, sugar, dried oregano, red pepper flakes, and a big pinch of salt. Bring to a simmer and cook, stirring occasionally, until most of the excess tomato juice has evaporated and the sauce has thickened, about 15 minutes. Remove from the heat and set aside to cool at room temperature.

5. Thirty minutes before you're ready to bake the pizzas, put a large inverted baking sheet onto the lowest oven rack and preheat the oven to 475°F / 245°C.

6. Soak the sliced jalapeño in a small bowl of ice water for 30 minutes. Drain and dry well with paper towels. This will help cut the heat of the jalapeño and ensure it does not burn in the hot oven.

7. Once the dough balls have doubled in size, place a large piece of parchment paper on a flat work surface. Place one dough ball in the center of the parchment paper and use your hands to stretch and press the dough into an 11-inch / 28cm round. Brush the dough all over with 1 tablespoon of the remaining olive oil. Spread half of the tomato sauce onto the dough, leaving a ½-inch / 1.3cm border, then scatter half of the mozzarella and provolone on top of the sauce. Sprinkle with 1 tablespoon of the remaining Parmesan, then top evenly with half of the Canadian bacon, pineapple, and sliced jalapeños.

8. Transfer the pizza (with the parchment paper) onto a second inverted large baking sheet, then slide the pizza (with the parchment paper) onto the hot inverted baking sheet in the oven. Bake for 10 minutes, then turn on the oven light and check on the pizza. Do not open the oven door, which will lower the oven temperature. The pizza crust should be puffed and deeply golden brown and the cheese should be completely melted and browned in spots. If the pizza looks like this, remove it from the oven. If not, continue baking the pizza for 2 to 5 more minutes (the exact cook time will depend heavily on your oven).

9. Let the baked pizza cool for a couple of minutes before slicing into wedges and serving immediately. Repeat to form and bake the second pizza.

> **"I STILL HIGHLY RECOMMEND SLAPPING SOME JUICY PINEAPPLE ON YOUR PIE. OH, FRUIT ON YOUR PIZZA IS GNARLY, YOU SAY? WELL, I SAY TRY BEFORE YOU DENY."**
>
> **ARGYLE**

Surfer Boy
Pizza
PAGE 162

Murray's Risotto

SERVES 4 TO 6 (A SCANT 6 CUPS / 1300G)

He can cook. He can clean. He speaks Russian and knows karate. What can't *Murray Bauman do? When he shows up, at Joyce's request, at the Byers home in California, Murray comes bearing gifts, specifically this "schmackin'" risotto he prepares for a (very high) Jonathan and Argyle, a somewhat confused El, Will, and Mike, and a grateful Joyce. As Murray, a former investigative journalist, would tell you, the secret is to keep stirring the pot.*

3 large sprigs fresh thyme

2 dried bay leaves

7 cups / 1.7L low-sodium chicken stock or vegetable stock

2 tablespoons extra-virgin olive oil, plus more for drizzling

1 large shallot, finely chopped (about ½ cup / 80g)

Kosher salt and freshly ground black pepper

4 garlic cloves, minced

¼ cup / 55g unsalted butter, divided

1¾ cups / 350g Arborio rice

¾ cup / 175ml dry white wine

1 cup / 100g freshly grated Parmesan cheese, plus more for sprinkling

Celery salt, for sprinkling (optional)

2 to 3 tablespoons sliced fresh chives

"THIS RISOTTO IS SCHMACKIN', DUDE."

ARGYLE

1. Tie the thyme sprigs together with kitchen twine, then combine with the bay leaves and stock in a medium saucepan. Set over medium heat until it comes to a simmer, about 10 minutes, then reduce the heat to low, cover with a lid, and keep warm while you start on the risotto.

2. In a large high-sided skillet over medium heat, warm the olive oil until it shimmers. Add the shallot, a large pinch of salt, and several grinds of black pepper and cook, stirring occasionally, until tender, about 5 minutes. Add the garlic and cook, stirring constantly, until softened, about 2 minutes.

3. Add 2 tablespoons of the butter and cook, stirring constantly, until melted, about 1 minute.

4. Add the rice, season with a large pinch of salt, and toast, stirring occasionally, until it smells nutty and starts to turn light golden brown in spots, about 5 minutes. Pour in the wine and simmer, stirring occasionally, until it has evaporated completely, 2 to 3 minutes.

5. Ladle 1 cup / 240ml of the warm stock into the rice and cook, stirring constantly, until the rice has absorbed the liquid, 2 to 3 minutes.

6. Repeat this process, adding more stock, a scant cup at a time, until the rice is al dente, about 20 additional minutes. You may have a little bit of stock left over, but that is okay, and you can use it to loosen up the cooked risotto as needed.

7. Add the Parmesan and the remaining 2 tablespoons butter and stir vigorously until the butter and cheese are melted and the risotto is nice and creamy, about 1 minute. Adjust the risotto to your liking by stirring in a splash or two of the remaining stock and season with more salt and pepper if needed. Divide the risotto among four to six shallow serving bowls, drizzle with more olive oil, and sprinkle generously with additional Parmesan and a dash of celery salt (if using). Top the risotto with the sliced chives and serve immediately.

Concession Stand Popcorn

MAKES 12 BARS

It's 1986 and video is king. Nothing is better than cozying up on the couch and inserting your rental VHS cassette into the VCR, with its satisfying electronic gulp. As bona fide movie nerds, Steve and Robin have passed many days at the Family Video counter watching the year's new releases, like Back to the Future *and* National Lampoon's European Vacation. *They enjoy each other's company, but the most important accompaniment is this decadent popcorn mix, with the entire concession aisle offerings folded in.*

Cooking spray
2 tablespoons canola oil
⅓ cup / 65g popcorn kernels
2 tablespoons unsalted butter
1 (10-ounce / 283g) bag mini marshmallows
Pinch of kosher salt
¾ cup / 90g salted roasted peanuts
¾ cup / 35g lightly crushed potato chips
½ cup / 100g candy-coated chocolate candies

COOK'S NOTE Instead of popping your own popcorn, you can use about 9 cups / 75g pre-popped bagged or microwave popcorn instead. Just skip the salt in the recipe, as the pre-popped or microwave popcorn will most likely already have salt in it.

1. Lightly coat a 9 by 13-inch / 24 by 36cm baking dish with cooking spray and set aside.

2. In a wide, high-sided pot over medium-high heat, warm the canola oil. When the oil starts to shimmer, add the popcorn kernels and stir to coat. Cover with a lid and turn off the heat for 1 minute; this allows all the kernels to get to the same temperature without the risk of burning.

3. Turn the heat to medium and listen closely until you hear the first couple of kernels pop, 1 to 2 minutes. Give the pot a good shake and then continue cooking with the lid just barely ajar to allow steam to escape, gently shaking the pot occasionally, until the popping slows down significantly, 2 to 3 minutes more. Turn off the heat and transfer the popcorn to a large glass or metal bowl and set aside.

4. Carefully wipe out the pot, add the butter, and return to medium heat. Once the butter is melted, add the marshmallows and salt and cook, stirring frequently, until the marshmallows are completely melted and the mixture is smooth, about 3 minutes. Scrape the marshmallow mixture over the popcorn and stir to combine. Then add the peanuts and potato chips and fold into the popcorn. Working quickly, put half of the mixture into the prepared baking dish and gently press down until mostly flat. Sprinkle with half of the chocolate candies and then top with the remaining popcorn mixture. Gently press the popcorn so it is flat (but not too compressed, as that will make it hard to eat) and then sprinkle with the remaining candies. Gently press the candies into the popcorn. Let sit at room temperature for 20 minutes.

5. When ready to serve, remove the popcorn treats from the baking dish, lightly coat a serrated knife with cooking spray, and cut into twelve large bars.

Kamchatka Feast

After subsisting on gruel and hard black bread, the prisoners at the Kamchatka penal colony are beside themselves with joy when they are led to a table laden with delicacies. All, that is, except Hopper, who cannily guesses why they're being fattened. But you don't have to be a prisoner in the Soviet gulag about to face off with the terrifying Demogorgon to enjoy a Russian feast. Originally made by a French chef for a noble Russian family (the Stroganovs) in the nineteenth century, Beef Stroganoff includes cognac, cream, and rib eye steak. Pirozhki, on the other hand, are Russia's famous cabbage-stuffed dumplings, as comforting a food as any, often made by babushkas and served with love and a sizable amount of vodka.

Beef Stroganoff

SERVES 4 TO 6

Kosher salt

2 (8-ounce / 225g) boneless rib eye steaks (1 inch / 2.5cm thick)

2 tablespoons vegetable oil

Freshly ground black pepper

6 tablespoons / 85g unsalted butter, divided

8 ounces / 225g cremini mushrooms, sliced about ¼ inch / 6mm thick

4 ounces / 115g shiitake mushrooms, sliced about ¼ inch / 6mm thick

2 shallots, finely diced

3 garlic cloves, minced

2 teaspoons finely chopped fresh thyme

⅓ cup / 80ml cognac

1 tablespoon all-purpose flour

1 cup / 240ml beef stock

12 ounces / 340g wide or extra-wide egg noodles

3 tablespoons chopped fresh flat-leaf parsley leaves, divided

¾ cup / 180g crème fraîche, at room temperature

1 tablespoon Dijon mustard

1 tablespoon soy sauce

174

1. Bring a large stockpot of salted water to a boil. Cut the steaks crosswise against the grain into ½-inch / 1.3cm-thick slices.

2. While the water comes to a boil, in a large cast-iron skillet over medium-high heat, warm the vegetable oil and swirl the skillet to coat. Season the steak slices liberally with salt and pepper. When the oil starts to shimmer, add half of the steak in a single layer and sear on both sides until deeply browned but still medium to medium-rare in the center, about 1 minute per side. Transfer to a large plate and repeat with the remaining steak.

3. Once all the steak is browned, melt 2 tablespoons of the butter in the empty skillet. Add the cremini and shiitake mushrooms and cook, stirring frequently, until nicely browned, about 10 minutes. Add 1 tablespoon of the remaining butter and the shallots, season with salt and pepper, and cook, stirring frequently, until tender, 3 to 5 minutes. Add the garlic and thyme and cook, stirring constantly, until softened, 1 to 2 minutes more. Turn off the heat and carefully add the cognac. Stir to combine and then turn the heat to medium. Cook, stirring constantly, until the cognac has mostly absorbed into the vegetables, about 2 minutes.

4. Sprinkle the flour into the skillet and cook, stirring constantly, for 1 minute. Stir in the beef stock and simmer, stirring occasionally, until the sauce is thickened to the consistency of thin gravy, 6 to 8 minutes.

5. Meanwhile, add the egg noodles to the boiling water and cook until al dente, 5 to 7 minutes. Reserve ½ cup / 120ml of the cooking water and then drain the noodles. In a large bowl, toss the hot noodles with the remaining 3 tablespoons butter and 2 tablespoons of the parsley and season with salt and pepper. Cover with aluminum foil to keep warm.

6. When the sauce has thickened, stir in the crème fraîche, mustard, and soy sauce and bring back to a simmer. Add the seared steak and any accumulated meat juices and cook until heated through, 1 to 2 minutes. Season with salt and pepper if needed. If the sauce is a bit too thick, add a splash of the reserved noodle cooking water to thin it out.

7. Divide the egg noodles among four to six bowls (or serve family style on a large platter) and top with the sauce and steak. Garnish with the remaining 1 tablespoon parsley and serve immediately.

Cabbage Pirozhki

MAKES 12 PIROZHKI

⅔ cup / 160ml milk, divided

1 tablespoon granulated sugar

1¾ teaspoons active dry yeast

3 large eggs

1 large egg yolk

¼ cup / 60g sour cream

¼ cup / 60ml canola oil, plus more for greasing and frying

Kosher salt

3 cups / 420g all-purpose flour, divided, plus more for dusting

2 tablespoon unsalted butter

1 small yellow onion, finely chopped

Freshly ground black pepper

2 garlic cloves, minced

12 ounces / 340g green cabbage (about half of a small head), cored and finely shredded

1½ tablespoons finely chopped fresh dill

1. Pour half of the milk into a small bowl and heat in the microwave until it is lukewarm (around 110°F / 43°C). Sprinkle the sugar and yeast over the lukewarm milk and stir to combine. Set aside until the yeast is frothy and bubbly, about 10 minutes.

2. In a large bowl, whisk together the remaining milk, one egg, the egg yolk, sour cream, canola oil, and 2 teaspoons salt until smooth. Add the yeast mixture and whisk to combine. Add half of the flour and stir with a rubber spatula or wooden spoon until just combined. Add the remaining flour and stir until a shaggy dough forms. Use your hands to knead the dough several times in the bowl until the dough comes together into a rough dough ball. On a heavily floured work surface, knead the dough until it is smooth and supple, 2 to 3 minutes, dusting with more flour if needed.

3. Wipe out the large bowl you made the dough in and grease it with additional oil. Add the dough, turn to coat in the oil, then cover the bowl with plastic wrap. Set aside at room temperature until the dough doubles in size, 1½ to 2 hours.

4. Meanwhile, bring a small saucepan of water to a boil. Use a large slotted spoon to gently lower the two remaining eggs into the boiling water. Cook for 12 minutes. While the eggs cook, fill a medium bowl with ice water.

5. After 12 minutes, transfer the eggs to the ice water and let sit until completely cooled. Once cooled, peel and coarsely chop the eggs. Set aside.

6. In a large skillet over medium heat, melt the butter. Once it is foamy, add the onion, season with salt and pepper, and cook, stirring occasionally, until tender, 6 to 8 minutes. Stir in the garlic and cook, stirring constantly, until softened, about 1 minute. Add the cabbage, season with salt and pepper, and cook, stirring occasionally, until wilted and tender (but not mushy), 10 to 12 minutes. Remove from the heat and season with additional salt and pepper if needed. Transfer to a medium bowl and stir in the chopped hard-boiled eggs and dill. Chill the filling in the refrigerator until you are ready to assemble the pirozhki.

7. Once the dough has doubled in size, line a large baking sheet with parchment paper and set aside.

8. Lightly dust a flat work surface with flour, punch down the risen dough, and turn the dough out onto the work surface. Cut the dough into four equal pieces. Keep one piece of the dough on the work surface, then wrap up the remaining dough and chill in the refrigerator. Fill a small bowl with cold water and set by your work surface.

9. Cut the one piece of dough into three equal portions. Roll each portion into a small dough ball. Lightly dust a rolling pin and roll one dough ball into a 5-inch / 13cm round that is about ⅛ inch / 3mm thick. Spoon 2 heaping tablespoons of the chilled cabbage filling in the center of the dough round. With a pastry brush or your fingers, brush cold water along the edge of half of the dough. the round, then bring the two sides of the dough together at the top of the filling to resemble a pouch or purse. Use your fingers to firmly pinch the dough together so that the pirozhki is tightly sealed from edge to edge, squeezing out any air from around the filling.

10. Place the formed pirozhki onto the prepared baking sheet seam-side up and cover with a clean kitchen towel. Roll, fill, and shape the two remaining dough balls. Once the first three pirozhki are formed, move the baking sheet to the refrigerator and continue forming the remaining dough to make additional pirozhki. Continue to transfer the formed pirozhki to the baking sheet in the refrigerator.

11. Once all of the pirozhki are formed, fill a large high-sided skillet with 1 inch / 2.5cm of oil and heat to 350°F / 175°C over medium-high heat. Line a large baking sheet or platter with several layers of paper towels. When the oil is up to temperature, lower four of the pirozhki into the hot oil, seam-side down, and cook until the dough is puffed, golden brown, and cooked through, 4 to 5 minutes, turning the pirozhki frequently so that the dough cooks evenly. Transfer to the paper towel–lined baking sheet or platter and fry the remaining pirozhki.

12. Serve immediately while the pirozhki are warm.

Hideout Hamburger Helper

SERVES 4

Supplies are low at Reefer Rick's dock house, where a terrified Eddie Munson is hiding out. Just a couple of unidentified boxes and cans in the pantry stand between Eddie and hunger. Thankfully, one of them is that staple of pantries across the country, Hamburger Helper. As Eddie waits for his friends to deliver supplies, he makes do. And as far as last meals go, this delicious mixture of ground beef and pasta isn't so bad.

1 tablespoon canola oil
1 pound / 450g lean ground beef
Kosher salt and freshly ground black pepper
1 yellow onion, coarsely chopped
3 tablespoons tomato paste
2 teaspoons garlic powder
1½ teaspoons paprika
1 tablespoon Worcestershire sauce
3 cups / 720ml beef stock
3 cups / 263g elbow macaroni pasta
4 ounces / 115g cream cheese, cut into 6 pieces
2 cups / 240g shredded sharp cheddar cheese

1. In a large pot or Dutch oven set over medium-high heat, warm the canola oil until it starts to shimmer. Add the ground beef, season with salt and pepper, and cook, using a wooden spoon to break up the meat, until browned and cooked through, 6 to 8 minutes. Add the onion and cook, stirring frequently, until tender, 5 to 7 minutes. Stir in the tomato paste, garlic powder, and paprika and cook, stirring constantly, for 2 minutes more. Add the Worcestershire sauce and beef stock, season with salt and pepper, stir to combine, and bring to a boil. Stir in the macaroni and then turn the heat down to maintain a simmer. Cover and cook until the pasta is al dente, about 8 minutes.

2. Remove the lid and turn the heat down to low. Add the cream cheese and stir until the sauce is smooth and creamy. Add the cheddar, a handful at a time, stirring after each addition and allowing the cheese to melt completely before adding more. Season with salt and pepper. If the sauce seems a touch thin, remove the pot from the heat and let it sit at room temperature for a couple of minutes, then give it a good stir.

3. Scoop the mixture into bowls and serve immediately.

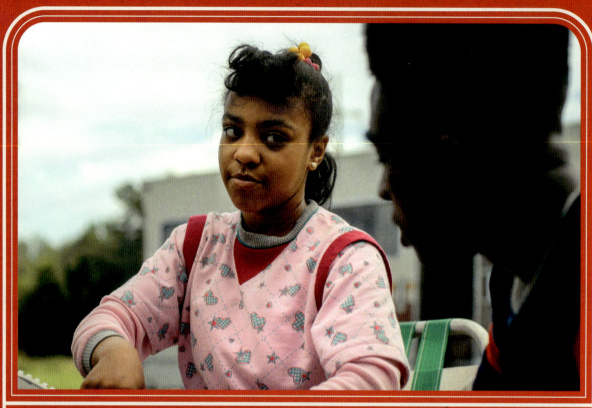

The
Sinclairs'
Banana Cream
Pudding
PAGE 182

The Sinclairs' Banana Cream Pudding

SERVES 8 TO 12

Every family has their celebration cake. For the Sinclairs, it's this achingly sweet and irresistible banana cream pudding. When Erica brings home a straight A+ report card (which is often), it's banana cream pudding. When Lucas wins the championship basketball game (which has only happened once), it's banana cream pudding. It's both a reward and an incentive and one of the Sinclairs' most treasured recipes.

5 cups / 1.2L whole milk

1 cup / 200g granulated sugar

6 tablespoons / 50g cornstarch

¾ teaspoon kosher salt

2 cups / 475ml heavy cream, divided

6 egg yolks

⅓ cup / 80ml crème de banana (see Cook's Note)

8 ounces / 226g cream cheese, cut into 8 pieces, divided, at room temperature

1½ tablespoons vanilla extract, divided

5 large ripe bananas, divided

¼ cup / 30g confectioners' sugar

75 vanilla wafers, divided

1. In a large saucepan, warm the milk over medium heat, stirring occasionally, until it just starts to steam, 6 to 8 minutes. Turn off the heat.

2. In a large bowl, whisk together the granulated sugar, cornstarch, and salt until well combined. Add ½ cup / 120ml of the heavy cream and the egg yolks and whisk until smooth. Slowly whisk half of the hot milk into the egg mixture until smooth. Gradually whisk the egg-milk mixture into the saucepan with the rest of the hot milk. Turn the heat to medium and cook, whisking constantly, until the mixture starts to bubble, about 20 minutes. Be patient with this step and do not be tempted to raise the heat; the pudding needs to cook slowly over moderate heat to thicken without scorching.

3. Once the pudding starts to bubble pretty vigorously, add the crème de banana and continue to cook, whisking constantly, until it has thickened to a pudding-like consistency, about 5 minutes more. Remove from the heat and add six pieces (6 ounces / 170g) of the cream cheese and 1 tablespoon of the vanilla and whisk until the cream cheese melts into the pudding and the mixture is completely smooth.

4. Transfer the pudding into a medium bowl. Place a piece of plastic wrap directly on top of the pudding and let cool at room temperature for 15 minutes, then transfer to the refrigerator and let chill for 45 minutes. It will not be fully chilled at this point (it might even still be warm), but that is okay. It just needs to be cooled down enough so it's not screaming hot when it gets layered with the bananas and vanilla wafers.

5. When the pudding is about 5 minutes away from coming out of the refrigerator, peel four of the bananas and thinly slice on a slight bias about ¼ inch / 6mm thick. In the bottom of a 9 by 13-inch / 24 by 36cm baking dish, spread 1½ cups / 360ml of the chilled pudding. Layer with half of the banana slices, 35 vanilla wafers, 1½ cups / 360 ml pudding, the remaining banana slices, 1½ cups / 360ml pudding, 35 vanilla wafers, and the remaining pudding. Cover with plastic wrap and refrigerate until the pudding is completely chilled and a long wooden skewer goes through the pudding without any resistance (this means that the cookies have softened completely), at least 6 hours or up to overnight.

6. When ready to serve, in a large bowl, combine the remaining two pieces (2 ounces / 55g) of cream cheese, the confectioners' sugar, and remaining 1½ teaspoons vanilla. Using an electric handheld mixer on medium speed, blend until completely smooth and combined. Add ½ cup / 120ml of the remaining heavy cream and blend again until smooth, then add the remaining 1 cup / 240ml heavy cream. Blend on low speed until the ingredients are incorporated, then whip on medium-high speed until medium-stiff peaks form. Set aside.

7. Peel and cut the remaining banana into ¼-inch / 6mm-thick slices. Spread the whipped cream on top of the pudding and then nestle the sliced bananas into the whipped cream. Coarsely crumble the remaining five vanilla wafers and sprinkle over the bananas.

COOK'S NOTE

Crème de banana is a sweet banana-flavored liqueur with a golden hue. Choose one that has an alcohol content no higher than 30 percent, because anything above that might cause the pudding to curdle. You can substitute 2 teaspoons banana extract for the liqueur; add it with the cream cheese and vanilla extract.

Yuri's Peanut Butter Blossoms

MAKES 24 COOKIES

A man will do a lot for freedom and smuggled goods, as the slippery Yuri shows. In his church, a sanctuary for his contraband, Yuri stockpiles boxes of peanut butter, a delectable Western treat unknown in Mother Russia. And when things are really going well, when all his schemes are working out just right, Yuri enjoys these sweet (and very Western) cookies. Sugar, butter, peanut butter, Hershey's Kisses—each ingredient is precious and rare, something that makes these cookies even more delicious.

1½ cups / 210g all-purpose flour
¾ teaspoon baking soda
½ teaspoon baking powder
½ teaspoon kosher salt
⅔ cup / 130g granulated sugar, divided
½ cup / 100g packed light brown sugar
½ cup / 110g unsalted butter, at room temperature
2 tablespoons honey
½ cup / 120g crunchy peanut butter
1 egg
24 drop-shaped milk chocolate candies, such as Hershey's Kisses

1. In a medium bowl, whisk together the flour, baking soda, baking powder, and salt. Set aside.

2. In a large bowl, combine ⅓ cup / 65g of the granulated sugar and the brown sugar, butter, and honey. Using a handheld mixer on low speed, incorporate the ingredients, then turn the speed to medium-high and blend until pale and fluffy, about 5 minutes, scraping down the bowl as needed. Add the peanut butter and egg and mix until smooth and creamy, about 1 minute more. Add the flour mixture and mix on low speed until just combined, scraping down the bowl as needed. Cover the bowl with plastic wrap and let chill in the refrigerator for 1 hour.

3. Preheat the oven to 375°F / 190°C. Line two baking sheets with parchment paper. Put the remaining ⅓ cup / 65g granulated sugar into a small bowl.

4. Portion about half of the chilled dough into twelve balls (a scant 1 ounce / 30g each) and roll evenly in the sugar. After all the dough balls have been rolled once in the sugar, roll each a second time and then arrange, spaced evenly apart, on one of the prepared baking sheets. Place the unportioned dough back in the refrigerator.

5. Bake, rotating the baking sheet 180 degrees halfway through, until the cookies are crackly and lightly browned in spots but still appear slightly underdone in the center, about 10 minutes. Remove from the oven and immediately press a chocolate candy into the center of each cookie. Let the cookies cool on the baking sheet for 5 minutes and then transfer to a wire rack to cool completely.

6. As the first batch of cookies is cooling, roll the remaining dough into twelve more balls, double-coat in the sugar, and arrange on the second baking sheet. Repeat the baking and cooling process.

7. Once cooled, serve the cookies immediately or transfer to an airtight container and store at room temperature for up to 5 days.

Victor Creel's Calming Whiskey Sour

SERVES 1

When the Creels moved to Morehead Street in 1959, everything seemed right as rain. The Creels—Victor, his wife, Virginia, and their two children, Henry and Alice—settled in to the elegant Victorian mansion. Many nights, Victor would spend the evening after dinner in the den, calming his frayed nerves with his favorite drink, a whiskey sour, to which Virginia added a soothing homemade ginger-honey-chamomile tincture. Alas, the Creels had only one month of peace before misfortune would visit their house, sending Ginny and Alice to their deaths, Henry into the Upside Down, and Victor to Pennhurst Mental Hospital.

2 ounces / 60ml whiskey or bourbon
1 ounce / 30ml Sleepy Time Syrup (recipe follows)
¾ ounce / 20ml fresh lemon juice
1 lemon wheel, for garnish
1 maraschino cherry, for garnish

COOK'S NOTE

To make a nonalcoholic version of this drink, use 2 ounces / 60ml chilled strongly brewed decaf black tea in place of the whiskey. Top with a splash of plain seltzer if you want to make the mocktail bubbly.

1. In a cocktail shaker filled with ice, combine the whiskey, Sleepy Time Syrup, and lemon juice. Cover the shaker and shake vigorously until the cocktail is well chilled.

2. Fill an old-fashioned or rocks glass with additional ice and strain the cocktail into the glass. Garnish with the lemon wheel and maraschino cherry. Serve immediately.

Sleepy Time Syrup

MAKES ABOUT ¾ CUP / 175ML

½ cup / 120ml water
½ cup / 120ml honey
One 2-inch / 5cm piece ginger, peeled and thinly sliced
4 chamomile tea bags (paper tags/labels removed)

1. In a small saucepan over medium heat, stir together the water, honey, and ginger and bring to a simmer, stirring occasionally, about 5 minutes. Remove from the heat and add the tea bags. Cool completely at room temperature.

2. Once cooled, strain the syrup through a fine-mesh sieve into a small bowl and press down on the ginger and tea bags to extract as much liquid as possible. Transfer the syrup into a glass jar. Use immediately or store in the refrigerator for up to 1 month.

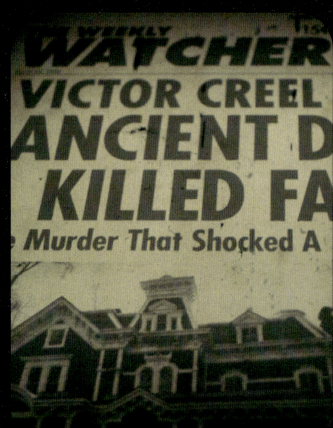

CHAPTER FIVE

19

87

AS THANKSGIVING APPROACHES, Hawkins in 1987 is a town torn apart and menaced. The destructive battle against Vecna has rent a giant scar through the center of town. Hawkins' residents are scared and anxious. Many have already left. The government has taken over, turning the once quiet Main Street into a corridor for military equipment. These are not normal times.

But it's also not anything the tough Hawkins kids can't handle. Trouble has chased the gang from the time they were in middle school. Now almost grown up, they know their own strength. Each is on their own journey, as they deal with the consequences of this fight and prepare for the next one. Dustin mourns Eddie. Lucas sits at Max's bedside in the hospital. Mike loves Eleven. Will loves Mike. Holly goes missing. Nancy and Jonathan are broken up. Hopper is single-mindedly focused on preparing El for the upcoming battle royale. And all this drama doesn't even factor in Vecna's plan to kidnap the children of Hawkins and take over the world.

This year, more than any before it, the gang has to come together and stay fortified for what promises to be a brutal last battle. Whether a tray of nachos or a grain bowl, food is the fuel that will keep Hawkins' heroes strong enough to fight. So, eat up—the world depends on it.

RECIPES

Karen Wheeler's Cheese-Pineapple Boats

SERVES 4

God bless Karen Wheeler, who has maintained a perfect perm and a cheerful demeanor in the face of nearly half a decade of mysterious and weird family drama. The Upside Down has both Holly and Mike. Her beloved Hawkins is now basically a military installation. Yet she still gets dinner on the table. And not just any dinner either. Karen continues to experiment with the greatest of contemporary '80s cuisine. Take, for instance, these delightful pineapple boats, a fruit salad and cheese plate mash-up disguised as a vessel, perhaps to ferry her family to happier, more peaceful times. And it works—during the meal, at least.

1 ripe pineapple with fresh green leaves

2 tablespoons granulated sugar

2 tablespoons fresh lime juice

1 (½-inch / 1.3cm) piece fresh ginger, peeled and finely grated (about 1 teaspoon)

4 ounces / 115g blackberries

6 ounces / 170g small strawberries, stems removed and quartered

¾ cup / 180g plain whole milk yogurt

2 tablespoons honey

2 tablespoons milk

½ teaspoon poppy seeds

2 ounces / 55g sharp cheddar cheese, cut into ½-inch / 1.3cm cubes

2 ounces / 55g provolone cheese, cut into ½-inch / 1.3cm cubes

¼ cup / 30g roasted hazelnuts, coarsely chopped

1. Use a serrated knife to cut the pineapple lengthwise (top to bottom) into quarters. The serrated knife will make it easier to cut through the thick green leaves. Switch over to a paring knife and carve out the pineapple flesh from the shells. Trim away the tough core and cut the pineapple into bite-size chunks (about 2 heaping cups / 335g). Reserve the shells. They are the pineapple "boats."

2. In a medium bowl, combine the sugar, lime juice, and ginger. Whisk until the sugar is dissolved, then spoon half of the mixture into a second medium bowl. Add the pineapple chunks into one bowl and the blackberries and strawberries into the second bowl. Stir both to combine, then chill in the refrigerator for 30 minutes. Give both bowls of fruit a good stir several times while they chill.

3. In a small bowl, combine the yogurt, honey, milk, and poppy seeds. Whisk until smooth. Chill in the refrigerator until ready to assemble the pineapple boats.

4. After 30 minutes, stir the cheddar and provolone cubes into the pineapple chunks. Use a slotted spoon to layer the dressed pineapple, cheese, and berries into the pineapple boats. Spoon the yogurt sauce over the fruit and cheese, sprinkle with the chopped hazelnuts, and serve immediately.

Byers-Style Classic Nachos

SERVES 4 TO 6 (ABOUT 3 CUPS / 680G)

With Jonathan almost all grown up and Will growing more distant every day, Joyce can feel the Byers household shifting beneath her feet. So Joyce does what she can to bring the family back together: movie night, just like she and Bob and the kids used to enjoy together. But even if the boys can't agree on which rental to bring home from Family Video (Jonathan wants Beverly Hills Cop II; *Will wants* Dirty Dancing)*, they can all agree that these nachos are the real stars of the show. They're topped with homemade nacho cheese and spiced with pickled jalapeños for an extra kick.*

3 tablespoons unsalted butter

3 tablespoons all-purpose flour

2 cups / 475ml whole milk, plus more as needed

Kosher salt

¼ teaspoon granulated garlic

⅛ to ¼ teaspoon cayenne pepper

4 ounces / 115g deli-style American cheese slices without plastic wrap (about 5 slices), cut into ½-inch / 1.3cm pieces (about 1 cup)

6 ounces / 170g mild cheddar cheese, grated (about 2½ cups)

8 ounces / 225g round corn tortilla chips (about 10 cups)

Pickled Jalapeños (recipe follows; optional)

1. In a medium saucepan over medium heat, melt the butter. Once the butter is melted, sprinkle the flour into the saucepan, whisk to combine, and cook until the flour is lightly toasted, about 3 minutes, whisking constantly.

2. While whisking constantly, slowly stream in the milk. Whisk in ½ teaspoon salt, the granulated garlic, and cayenne pepper and bring the milk to a simmer, about 5 minutes, whisking constantly. Once at a simmer, continue to cook, whisking constantly, until the mixture thickens, 1 to 2 additional minutes.

3. Remove the saucepan from the stovetop, add the American cheese, and whisk until the cheese is melted. Add the cheddar and whisk to combine (it will not be melted at this point), then return the saucepan to the stovetop and set it over low heat. Continue to whisk until the cheddar is melted and the sauce is smooth, about 2 minutes. If the sauce is super thick, whisk in additional milk, 1 tablespoon at a time, until it drizzles off of the whisk nicely. Season the nacho cheese with additional salt if needed.

4. Scatter half of the tortilla chips onto an extra-large flat platter (a large rimmed baking sheet also works well), drizzle half of the nacho cheese over the chips, scatter the remaining chips on top of the sauce, then drizzle with the remaining nacho cheese. Garnish with pickled jalapeños (if using) and serve immediately. Alternatively, you can serve the hot nacho cheese sauce in ramekins and serve on the side of four to six smaller plates of tortilla chips.

RECIPE CONTINUES >>>

Pickled Jalapeños

MAKES 1½ CUPS / 340G

3 large jalapeños (about 4 ounces / 115g), sliced
    into ⅛-inch / 3mm rounds (about 1½ cups)
½ cup / 120ml white distilled vinegar
⅓ cup / 80ml water
3 garlic cloves, lightly smashed
2 tablespoons granulated sugar
2 teaspoons kosher salt

1. Put the sliced jalapeños into a heatproof glass food storage jar (at least 12 ounces / 360ml) and set aside.

2. In a small saucepan over medium heat, whisk together the vinegar, water, garlic, sugar, and salt and heat until hot, steamy, and just starting to bubble, about 3 minutes. Pour the pickling liquid over the jalapeños, give the jar a little shimmy to make sure the jalapeños are submerged, then let cool to room temperature. Cover with a lid, transfer to the refrigerator, and chill until cold before serving.

3. Serve immediately or store in the refrigerator for up to 2 weeks.

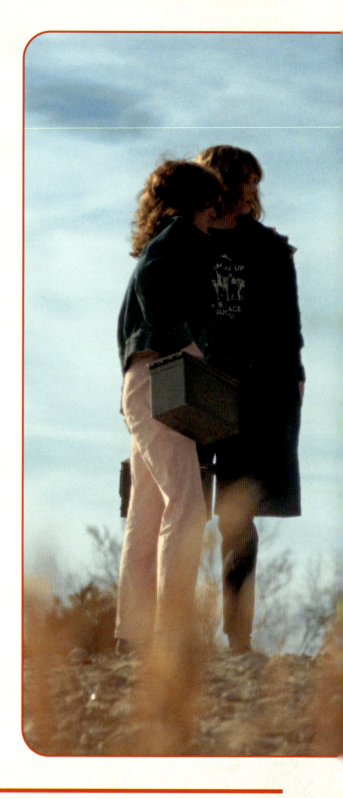

Mac-Z and Cheese

SERVES 6 TO 8

When the epic battle against Vecna tore a chasm through Hawkins in 1986, the military quickly occupied the town, reassuring Hawkins citizens they were just the unlucky survivors of an earthquake. The government's central hub of logistics is called the military action control zone, the Mac-Z for short. Most of the rations in the Mac-Z are standard-issue MREs, leaving soldiers hungry for home-cooked meals. Thanks to an inventive and kind mess hall leader, active duty personnel are treated to this rich Mac-Z and Cheese. It has all the comfort of a traditional mac and cheese but with the addition of cauliflower and sweet potatoes, for a little bit of a healthy edge.

Kosher salt

2 tablespoons unsalted butter

4 garlic cloves, thinly sliced

½ yellow onion, coarsely chopped

1 (12-ounce / 340g) can evaporated milk

½ cup / 120ml water

½ small head cauliflower, cut into florets

8 ounces / 225g sweet potatoes (about 1 large), peeled and cut into 1-inch / 2.5cm chunks

Freshly ground black pepper

1 pound / 450g elbow macaroni

1 teaspoon dry mustard powder

1½ cups / 180g shredded medium cheddar cheese

1½ cups / 180g shredded Colby Jack cheese

1 tablespoon cornstarch

1. Bring a large stockpot of salted water to a boil.

2. In a large high-sided skillet, melt the butter over medium heat. Add the garlic and onion and cook, stirring frequently, until tender, 6 to 8 minutes. Stir in the evaporated milk, water, cauliflower, sweet potato, 1½ teaspoons salt, and a couple grinds of black pepper. Bring to a boil, then lower the heat to maintain a simmer and cook, covered, stirring occasionally, until the vegetables are very tender, about 20 minutes.

3. Meanwhile, cook the elbow macaroni in the boiling water until al dente, about 5 minutes. Reserve 1 cup / 240ml of the pasta water, then drain the macaroni and set aside.

4. Once the vegetables are very tender (easily mashable), scoop the mixture (along with all of the cooking liquid) into a blender and add the mustard powder. Remove the cap from the lid, cover the small opening with a kitchen towel (this will help to release steam), and blend until completely smooth. Return the sauce to the skillet, stir in ¼ cup / 60ml of the reserved pasta water, and cook over medium heat until the sauce is steaming and lightly bubbling, stirring occasionally, about 2 minutes. In a medium bowl, combine the cheddar and Colby Jack. Sprinkle with the cornstarch and toss until evenly coated.

5. Add the cheese, a handful at a time, stirring well after each addition and allowing the cheese to melt completely before adding more. Once all of the cheese has been added to the sauce, cook, stirring constantly, until the mixture just starts to bubble, 2 to 4 minutes. Stir in the cooked macaroni and cook, stirring constantly, until the macaroni is heated through, 1 to 2 minutes more. If the sauce is too thick, stir in a splash of the reserved pasta water. Season with salt and pepper. Scoop into bowls and serve immediately.

Eleven-Ingredient Superpower Grain Bowl

SERVES 4

As Eleven trains emotionally, mentally, and physically for the biggest fight of her life, it's clear she is no longer the little girl who escaped from the Hawkins National Laboratory. The days of the Eggo Extravaganza are in the past; El now needs food that will sustain her battle against evil, like this grain bowl featuring superfoods, including kale, quinoa, edamame, and blueberries.

Quinoa and Marinated Kale

1 bunch Tuscan kale (about 10 ounces / 283g), stems removed, and leaves cut into roughly 1-inch / 2.5cm pieces (about 8 cups / 155g)

2 tablespoons extra-virgin olive oil, divided

Zest and juice from 1 small lemon (about 2 teaspoons zest and 2 tablespoons juice)

Kosher salt and freshly ground black pepper

1 cup / 180g raw tricolor quinoa, rinsed

3 tablespoons coarsely chopped flat-leaf parsley

Creamy Avocado Dressing

1 small ripe avocado (about 5 ounces / 140g)

Zest and juice from 1 large lemon (about 1 tablespoon zest and ¼ cup / 60ml juice)

½ cup / 120ml water, plus more as needed

¼ cup / 60ml extra-virgin olive oil

2 garlic cloves, finely grated

½ cup / 10g tightly packed fresh basil leaves

½ cup / 10g tightly packed fresh flat-leaf parsley leaves

Kosher salt and freshly ground black pepper

Assembly

1⅓ cups / 6 ounces steamed or grilled corn kernels (frozen and thawed sweet or fire-roasted corn works too)

1 cup / 140g cooked shelled edamame

1 cup / 115g fresh blueberries

1 small ripe Fuyu persimmon (about 5 ounces / 140g), peeled and cut into ¼-inch / 6mm wedges (about 1 scant cup / 115g)

4 ounces / 115g goat cheese, crumbled

¼ cup / 35g toasted and salted pepitas

2 tablespoons hulled hemp seeds

1. Make the quinoa and marinated kale: Put the sliced kale into a large bowl, drizzle with 1 tablespoon of the olive oil, half of the lemon juice, a large pinch of salt, and several grinds of black pepper. Use your hands to massage the kale until it wilts and becomes somewhat tender, about 2 minutes. Set aside while you prepare the quinoa.

2. Bring a large saucepan of lightly salted water to a boil over medium-high heat. Add the quinoa and cook until tender, about 15 minutes.

3. Drain the quinoa well in a large fine-mesh strainer and rinse with cold water until the quinoa is no longer warm. Shake the excess water from the chilled quinoa, then add it to the bowl with the marinated kale. Add the remaining 1 tablespoon olive oil, the lemon zest, and parsley, season with salt and pepper, and stir until well combined. Set aside while you make the dressing.

4. Make the creamy avocado dressing: Cut the avocado in half, remove the pit, and scoop the flesh into a blender carafe. Add the lemon juice, water, olive oil, garlic, basil, parsley, a large pinch of salt, and several large grinds of black pepper. Cover with the lid and blend until smooth. The dressing should be thick and creamy, but you can thin it out with additional water if desired. Season with additional salt and pepper if needed.

5. Assemble: Divide the quinoa and kale between four shallow bowls and top evenly with the corn, edamame, blueberries, persimmon wedges, crumbled goat cheese, and pepitas. Sprinkle each bowl with the hemp seeds and serve immediately with the creamy avocado dressing on the side.

Party Sandwich Loaf

SERVES 8 TO 12

To save the world, the Party will have to set aside their differences, rediscover the deep bonds of friendship that connect them, and work in harmony. Everyone will have to pitch in. Total participation in the campaign is mandatory. And each character adds their special flavor (Olive Nut Spread, Egg Salad, Deviled Ham Salad), working together (in a giant sandwich) enshrouded and ennobled by an impenetrable layer of friendship (garlic and herb cream cheese frosting). This loaf is a testament to friendship, to saving the world, and to lunch.

Olive-Nut Spread

½ cup / 50g raw shelled walnuts

½ cup / 50g pecans

6 ounces / 170g cream cheese, at room temperature

3 tablespoons mayonnaise

½ cup / 75g pimiento-stuffed green olives, finely chopped

Kosher salt and freshly ground black pepper

Egg Salad

6 eggs

⅓ cup / 80g mayonnaise

¼ cup / 30g finely diced celery

2 tablespoons finely diced red onion

1 tablespoon chopped fresh dill

1 tablespoon Dijon mustard

Kosher salt and freshly ground black pepper

Deviled Ham Spread

8 ounces / 225g smoked ham, coarsely chopped

3 tablespoons sour cream

3 tablespoons mayonnaise

2 teaspoons yellow mustard

¼ cup / 30g finely diced celery

2 tablespoons chopped fresh flat-leaf parsley leaves

2 tablespoons sweet pickle relish, drained well

2 tablespoons finely diced red onion

Dash of hot sauce

Kosher salt and freshly ground black pepper

Garlic and Herb Cream Cheese Frosting

½ cup / 10g packed fresh flat-leaf parsley leaves

¼ cup / 60ml half-and-half or heavy cream

1 teaspoon granulated garlic

1½ pounds / 680g cream cheese, at room temperature

To assemble

1 unsliced loaf of sandwich bread, ideally a square Pullman loaf

¼ cup / 55g salted butter, at room temperature

Fresh vegetables and herbs for decorations (such as radishes, carrots, cucumbers, dill, chives, flat-leaf parsley, and so on)

1. Make the olive-nut spread: Preheat the oven to 350°F / 175°C.

2. Scatter the walnuts and pecans onto a small baking sheet and toast in the oven until lightly browned and fragrant, 7 to 10 minutes, stirring the nuts several times to ensure they toast evenly. Transfer the nuts to a cutting board to cool completely, then chop very finely.

3. In a large bowl, combine the cream cheese and mayonnaise and stir until very smooth. Add the chopped pecans, walnuts, and olives and stir until well combined. Season with salt and pepper and set aside.

RECIPE CONTINUES >>>

4. Make the egg salad: Bring a large saucepan of water to a boil. Use a large slotted spoon to gently lower the eggs into the water and boil for 12 minutes. While the eggs cook, fill a large bowl with ice water.

5. After 12 minutes, transfer the eggs to the bowl of ice water and let sit until completely cool.

6. Meanwhile, in a medium bowl, stir together the mayonnaise, celery, onion, dill, and mustard. Peel and coarsely chop the eggs, add to the mayonnaise mixture, season with salt and pepper, and stir gently to combine. Chill in the refrigerator until ready to assemble the sandwich loaf.

7. Make the deviled ham spread: In a food processor, pulse the smoked ham until finely chopped. Add the sour cream, mayonnaise, and mustard and pulse until just combined. Transfer the mixture to a medium bowl and add the celery, parsley, relish, red onion, and hot sauce. Stir to combine. Season with salt and pepper and chill in the refrigerator until ready to assemble the sandwich loaf.

8. Make the herbed cream cheese frosting: In a blender, combine the parsley leaves, half-and-half or heavy cream, and granulated garlic. Blend until completely smooth and set aside.

9. In a large bowl, blend the cream cheese with an electric handheld mixer on medium-high speed until very smooth. Add the creamy herb mixture and blend until smooth and lightly fluffy.

10. Assemble: Trim the crusts from the bread loaf (if desired). Slice the loaf horizontally into four equal pieces. Lightly spread the butter on one side of the bottom three pieces. Spread a couple spoonfuls of the herbed cream cheese frosting onto a serving platter, then place the bottom bread piece on it, buttered-side up. Cover evenly with the olive-nut spread. Top with the second buttered bread piece, then cover with the deviled ham spread. Top with the third buttered bread piece, cover with the egg salad, then top with the unbuttered bread piece. Lightly press down on the assembled loaf (but be careful that none of the filling comes out) and chill in the refrigerator for 30 minutes.

11. After 30 minutes, spread the remaining herbed cream cheese frosting on the top and sides of the loaf. If desired, transfer some of the frosting to a piping bag fitted with a decorative tip and pipe a border around the bottom or top edges of the loaf. Decorate as you like with additional fresh vegetables and herbs. Lightly cover with plastic wrap and refrigerate for at least 4 hours and up to overnight.

12. Remove from the refrigerator, cut into 8 to 12 slices, and serve immediately.

Cranberry and Blood Orange Upside-Down Cake

SERVES 8 TO 10

The Upside Down has turned Hawkins upside down. The town and the world are saved only by the heroics of a group of friends and the mysterious Eleven. The last five years have been terrible in some ways but incredibly sweet in others. Friendships have deepened, hearts have opened, been broken, been healed. A group of young boys and girls have grown up and discovered that inside them is great strength and courage. What better way to capture this than with an upside-down cake that is decadent, blood-red, and triumphant?

2 cups / 475ml unsweetened cranberry juice

1½ cups / 300g granulated sugar, divided

¼ cup / 60ml pure maple syrup, plus more as needed

2 tablespoons cold unsalted butter, plus more for greasing

3 medium blood oranges

1⅓ cups / 185g all-purpose flour

½ cup / 75g medium-grind yellow cornmeal

2 teaspoons baking powder

½ teaspoon baking soda

1 teaspoon kosher salt

½ cup / 110g unsalted butter, at room temperature

2 tablespoons canola oil

2 eggs, at room temperature

1½ teaspoons vanilla extract

¾ cup / 175ml buttermilk, at room temperature

1. In a medium saucepan, combine the cranberry juice and ½ cup / 100g of the sugar and bring to a boil. Lower the heat to medium-low and cook, stirring occasionally, until reduced to ½ cup / 120ml, about 25 minutes. Transfer to a medium bowl and whisk in the maple syrup and the 2 tablespoons cold butter until smooth and combined. Set aside to cool slightly while you prepare the cake.

2. Preheat the oven to 350°F / 175°C. Generously butter a 9-inch / 23cm round cake pan, line the bottom with parchment paper, and butter the parchment paper.

3. Finely grate the zest from the blood oranges (about 1 tablespoon total) and set it aside. Working with one blood orange at a time, slice off the top and bottom and then sit the fruit upright on a cutting board. Slice along the curve of the fruit from the top to the bottom to remove the peel and pith. Slice the citrus crosswise into ¼-inch / 6mm-thick rounds. Repeat with the remaining oranges. Remove any seeds from the fruit.

4. Pour ⅓ cup / 80ml of the cranberry syrup (it will still be slightly warm and quite fluid at this point) into the prepared cake pan and swirl it around so it coats the bottom evenly. Top with the blood orange rounds so that they fit very snugly in a single layer and set the pan aside. Let the remaining cranberry syrup cool at room temperature. As it cools, it will set up similarly to a thick caramel sauce. The syrup will be tart, but you can whisk in additional maple syrup if you want it sweeter.

5. In a medium bowl, combine the flour, cornmeal, baking powder, baking soda, and salt and whisk to combine. In a large bowl, combine the ½ cup / 110g room-temperature butter, remaining 1 cup / 200g sugar, the orange zest, and canola oil. Using a handheld mixer on low speed, incorporate the ingredients, then turn the speed to medium-high and blend until pale and fluffy, about 5 minutes,

scraping down the bowl as needed. Add the eggs one at a time, beating well after each addition, then beat in the vanilla. Add half the flour mixture and mix until just combined, then add the buttermilk and mix again until almost combined (it does not need to be smooth). Add the remaining flour mixture and, using a rubber spatula, mix the batter by hand until just combined (do not overmix).

6. Gently spoon the batter into the prepared cake pan, being careful to not move the orange slices, and smooth the top. If some of the cranberry syrup comes up into the cake batter, that is okay; just gently swirl it into the batter. Place onto a baking sheet and bake, rotating the baking sheet 180 degrees after 30 minutes, until the top of the cake is golden brown and a wooden pick inserted into the center of the cake comes out clean, 40 to

45 minutes. Transfer the cake to a wire rack and immediately run a sharp knife around the edge of the cake. Let cool for 10 minutes and then carefully invert it onto a large platter or cake stand and gently remove the parchment paper. Let cool completely.

7. When ready to serve, slice the cake into thick wedges and drizzle with the remaining cranberry syrup.

Store any leftover cranberry syrup in an airtight container in the refrigerator for up to 2 weeks. To use, warm it ever so slightly in the microwave or on the stovetop until it easily drizzles off a spoon.

Vickie's Quickies Cherries Jubilee

SERVES 4

Despite the existential dangers menacing Hawkins, true love continues to blossom. Take Robin and Vickie, who finally have found each other. Theirs is a happy union that comforts Will as he accepts his identity. They show him what a relationship might look like, and over tea and desserts, like this easy-to-make one, they encourage him to show the world exactly who he is.

½ cup / 55g sliced almonds
2 tablespoons cold unsalted butter, divided
1 pound / 450g ripe sweet cherries, pitted
¼ cup / 50g granulated sugar
1 tablespoon fresh lemon juice
Pinch of kosher salt
¼ cup / 60ml cherry brandy (such as kirsch)
¼ cup / 90g cherry preserves
Vanilla ice cream, for serving
½ cup / 40g crumbled vanilla wafers

1. In a large skillet over medium heat, toast the almonds, tossing or stirring occasionally, until lightly browned in spots, 5 to 7 minutes. Transfer the almonds to a small bowl and set aside.

2. Return the skillet to medium heat and add 1 tablespoon of the butter. When the butter has melted and is foamy, add the cherries, sugar, lemon juice, and salt and cook, stirring occasionally, until the cherries are tender and the liquid has thickened into a syrupy glaze that clings to the fruit, 8 to 10 minutes.

3. Remove the skillet from the heat and add the cherry brandy. Ignite the alcohol with a long match or a stick lighter and gently swirl the pan until the flames subside, about 30 seconds.

4. Stir the remaining 1 tablespoon butter into the cherries until melted. Add the cherry preserves and stir again until melted into the sauce. Transfer to a medium bowl and let cool in the refrigerator for 20 minutes; the jubilee will thicken up slightly as it cools, but the sauce will still be a little warm at this point.

5. Fill four large sundae glasses halfway with scoops of vanilla ice cream. In each glass, layer ¼ cup of the cherries jubilee, 1 tablespoon almonds, 1 tablespoon crumbled vanilla wafers, and more ice cream, then top with additional cherries jubilee and garnish with the remaining almonds and vanilla wafers. Serve immediately.

ACKNOWLEDGMENTS

Like men and monsters, books too evolve, and this one has been no exception. The best part of my job is getting to work with people who are extremely good at theirs. My deepest gratitude to Sarah Malarkey at Random House Worlds, who has been a patient, kind, and apt shepherd along the way. Susan Vu, who developed all the recipes in this book, is exceptional and has been a perfect collaborator. This book is as much Susan Vu's as it is mine.

Just as a show has a cast (who you see) and a crew (who you don't), this book has relied on a team of dedicated and brilliant individuals. Among them are the food photographer Kristin Teig, who brought these food images so vibrantly to life with the help of Martha Bernabe (prop stylist) and Monica Pierini (food stylist); Laura Palese, who designed these pages, Jenny Davis (creative director), and Ian Dingman (art director); and Abby Duval (production editor) and Leda Scheintaub (copy editor), Demogorgons of grammar.

Fundamentally, this book couldn't have existed without the world created by the Duffer Brothers, their production partners at Netflix, and the entire cast and crew. Without them, the world of Hawkins (and the Upside Down) wouldn't have existed or been realized in such great detail so a cookbook could flow from it so easily.

Finally, a big thank you to my agent, David Black, without whom I'd be busy but aimless (and poorly compensated), and to my sons, Augustus and Achilles, whose presence in this world means every joke I make is a dad joke and is all the funnier.

INDEX

ABOUT THE AUTHOR

JOSHUA DAVID STEIN is a journalist, editor, and co-author of *The Nom Wah Cookbook* (with Wilson Tang), *Notes from a Young Black Chef* (with Kwame Onwuachi), *Il Buco: Stories and Recipes* (with Donna Lennard), and *Cooking for Your Kids,* as well as many children's books. Previously, Stein was the restaurant critic for *The Village Voice* and *The New York Observer.* He lives in Brooklyn with his two sons.

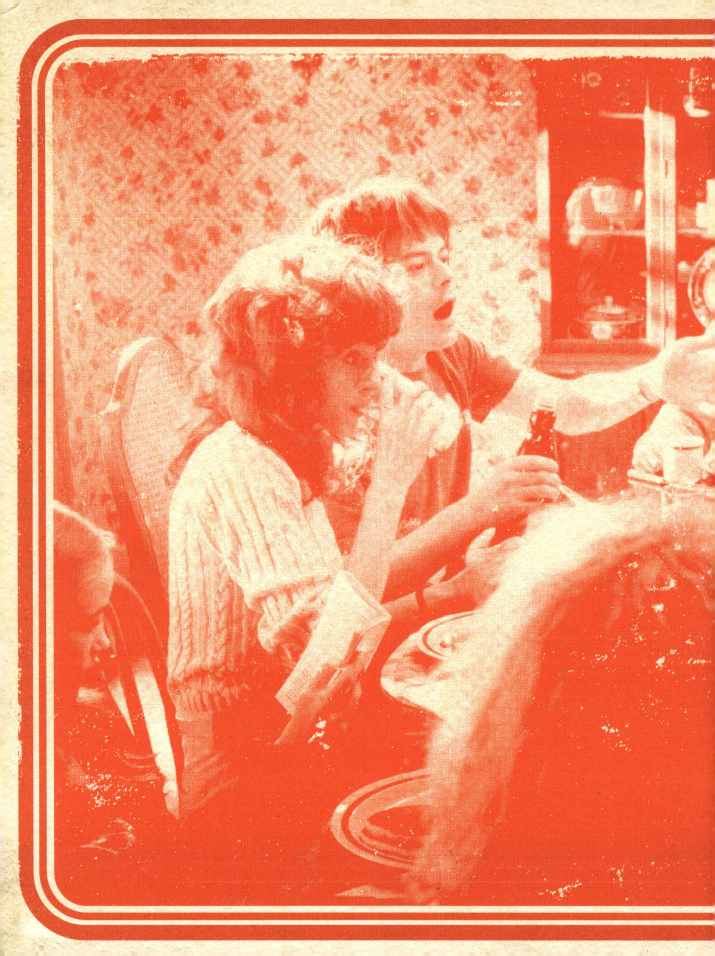